Unbraided

TRANSFORM YOUR PAIN
TO POWER AND PURPOSE

Unbraided

TRANSFORM YOUR PAIN
TO POWER AND PURPOSE

Karla Monterrosa

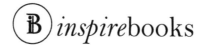

To the little girl who lost so much; as she runs to her Heavenly Father for the gift of life He has been holding for her all this time.

To my beloved husband and daughters, Gary, Aaliyah, and Alyssa—you taught me the meaning of unconditional love and inspired me to become the woman, wife, and mother you deserve.

CONTENTS

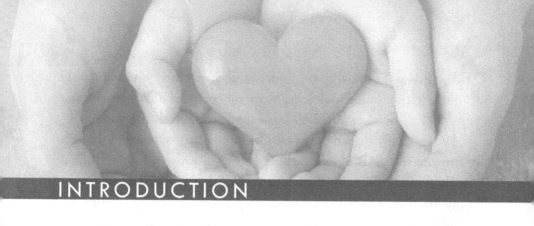

INTRODUCTION

I want to begin by congratulating you for your courage to open this book. The topic of childhood sexual abuse is a difficult and uncomfortable one, especially if you have experienced it yourself. As you know, those memories stay with us, sometimes only partially, but remain difficult to revisit. It is important, however, for us to courageously reflect, analyze, and feel through those memories in order to experience healing. When left unaddressed, those traumatic experiences influence our view of ourselves, how we respond to life's challenges, and how we either relate to or distance ourselves from each other. There isn't a single thing in our lives that isn't perceived through the sense of the victimization we experienced.

If you were sexually abused as a child, or experienced other forms of abuse in your childhood or adult life, there are areas in your life that are being affected right now by your trauma and you may not yet know it. Once you are aware, you can begin to take steps to change this. Once you are aware of the power those emotional and spiritual wounds have over you, you can begin to do something about them.

Perhaps you find yourself well-aware, tired, and hurting but don't know how to get free from your past. Or perhaps you have pushed your pain so far under the rug that you are comfortable with it and don't really want to bring it out and think about it again. You may be thinking, *Do I really want to read this book and have to deal with this?* I know it can feel heavy, but as with anything that involves work and struggle, the reward at the other side is so worth it.

I want you to know that I understand. I was there once, and only through self-reflection did I begin to connect the dots between my painful past and the struggles I was experiencing in the present.

I was sexually abused by people I knew and trusted between the ages of five and ten years old. The abuse I suffered early in my life turned my childhood into a set of dark memories that haunted me for most of my life. The experience left me feeling ashamed, angry, and unsafe.

When I grew up, for a time I was able to use the pain I felt as fuel. I achieved personal, educational, and professional successes thanks to that drive. I stood strong as an educated and professional woman. I was married and a mother to two beautiful little girls. I spent nearly twenty years working in government and helping to improve the lives of women and their families. Our household income exceeded six figures, and we owned a home in a quiet suburb in Los Angeles. Based on these achievements, I thought I had overcome the trauma I had experienced early in my life. I worked hard to break the cycle of abuse I was born into, and I thought I had won. I had built a life and a home that looked nothing like the one I was born into. I could see the darkness of my childhood experiences as a distant past, and yet freedom and healing eluded me. I didn't yet know it, but I was actually only halfway through the dark tunnel of my past—not on the other side as I had thought.

I had suppressed memories and ignored feelings, and fought to do the opposite of what I had seen in my childhood for nearly three decades. I had buried the feelings deep inside where I thought they could not hurt me anymore. In reality, I struggled with fear, anxiety, and an inability to trust people. For a long time, I didn't know these feelings were rooted in the abuse I experienced during my childhood. Meanwhile, they were influencing my life in insidious ways and affecting my relationships, my marriage and experience as a mother, and even my career. Eventually, I arrived at a season when I could no longer ignore my pain.

My efforts to silence the memories proved to be unsuccessful within the stresses and pressures of marriage and motherhood. It was then that my scars became utterly exposed. I came into the harsh realization that I had not healed when the memories relentlessly interrupted my time with my children. The day my daughter was born and I changed her first dirty diaper, I realized the abuse I suffered had wounded me profoundly and motherhood was going to be hard. Diaper changes and bath-time reminded me of how vulnerable children are. I struggled with this for years with both of my daughters. For sanitary reasons, those moments were unavoidable, and yet they made me feel dirty and ashamed, as though I were violating them when I cleaned and cared for them. I knew that was not what I should be thinking or feeling in those moments with my children, but I had no idea how to stop the thoughts from intruding in my life. It was a constant internal battle.

I struggled with memories, shame, fear, and a feeling of hyper-protection of my children. The unresolved pain I was still carrying inside started coming out as aggression. I was defensive and abrasive toward my husband and struggled to discipline my children with grace and patience. I could not control the circumstances that triggered my memories or my automatic responses to them. In moments of frustration, shame and anger dominated our interactions.

At the same time, I was giving everything at work, and it was never enough for those I reported to. I was exhausted. By the time I would arrive home at the end of my day, I would have nothing left to give but a bad temper, which affected our entire family dynamic. Eventually, I made a career move that brought my work closer to home in an attempt to have more time with my family. Unfortunately, the work environment there was such that I had to work extra-long hours to keep up the pace, which ultimately resulted in more stress and even less time and patience for my family. I wound up dissatisfied again. I had had enough but didn't know what I should do next. It was then that I humbly reached out to God for direction.

It started with the decision to take a break from my career. I knew in my heart for a long time that I was not walking in my purpose and needed the space to figure out what direction to take. Not knowing how we would sustain the lifestyle we had grown accustomed to, my husband and I made the bold decision to trust God fully for our financial provision, and I quit my job. The career that no longer satisfied me was in the rearview mirror, and I was ready to pursue new things. I decided to take some time to reflect and figure out what my next career move was going to be. It was within that space and that step of faith that God began to move and reveal himself. I started depending on Him for help and guidance. He started walking me through a process of healing.

I also recognized that my past was harming my family, and that was the greatest motivation for me to seek out true healing. I realized I would have to resolve my childhood wounds if I was going to successfully break the cycle of abuse and live a truly healthy life with my own family. That realization added to the desire in me. I wanted more than anything to finally be free from that trauma. And I had no idea how to go about it.

All I knew was I wanted more than anything to get to know God for who He truly is, to be present physically and emotionally for my family, and to align my work with my purpose. Little did I know, God was about to show me the reality and depth of the damage I still held onto and how desperately I needed Him. Once He began to connect the dots for me, I realized the darkness I experienced during childhood had grown tentacles and was clinging to every area of my being, silently suffocating all of the best things in my life.

Childhood abuse has deep and long-lasting effects that manifest themselves in subtle and devastating ways in our lives. Unless we know it, they remain a part of us, wreaking havoc. I had seen the signs and had my suspicions, but without the clarity of the Holy Spirit, I couldn't see it for what it indeed was.

One of the first things I did differently once I left my job was begin each day with God. I would drop my children off at school and come home to brew a pot of coffee and open my Bible. Through prayer, studying the Bible, and the unconditional love of the people around me, God began to walk me toward healing.

After a short break to focus on my girls and volunteer at their school, I began considering my next steps and decided to hire professional support to do so. I wanted to make the most of my time away from the workforce, and working with a coach provided me with guidance, reassurance, and an environment of discovery. It didn't take long for me to decide I would pursue my life-long dream of becoming a published author. I always knew I would share my story with the world one day. God revealed this to me long ago. I don't recall exactly when I first sensed or received that direction, but I have been thinking about this book for years.

What do I mean when I say I "received direction" from God? How do I know if a thought is my own or inspired by the one true God? For me, it can come as a subtle nudge to say or do something, or an all-out clear instruction to change course.

You may have already had an experience in your life where you knew God was trying to tell you something. You may know it as your subconscious, a gut feeling, intuition, or an "Aha! moment." Sometimes you listen to it. Other times you ignore it and then think, "I should have listened to my intuition." As Christians, we believe those "Aha! moments" are, in fact, the voice of God or the Holy Spirit. The Holy Spirit is a gift from God that allows us to see and think in new ways.

God's voice comes to me in whispers I know are not my own. I know these thoughts are not mine because they address things I have been thinking about without having clear direction on my own of what to do. I recognize His voice because He quiets my fears, answers my questions, and brings peace where there was doubt. The Bible tells us that when we draw near to God, He comes near to us (James 4:8). The more we seek His voice, the more clearly we are able to discern it. As we deepen our walk with God, we grow in wisdom and are able to see more clearly the things that make us feel separated from God and those that bring us closer to Him. The voice of God had been quietly urging me to write my story and share it with the world.

I was first introduced to Jesus as a child. At the time, I desperately needed a Savior to help me out of the fear and confusion that was dominating my life and my family. I accepted Him and held onto Him as my Savior for most of my life, but I didn't fully grasp or experience all that He offers us until recently. When I first found my faith, I did not receive a full representation of His grace and nature. I lived many years with a misconception of who He is and what He accomplished when He died for us on the cross. I learned an incomplete perspective of what it meant to choose and follow Jesus. I struggled to stick with my new-found faith for years but didn't feel good enough. I thought I would never live up to the man-made standards I had learned, and my on-and-off relationship with Him began.

I am not a psychologist or a theologically trained Bible teacher. I am a flawed individual with a history of abuse and struggle, like most of us. I am also a woman who has recently come into an awareness of the Bible's relevance in my everyday life. I have discovered God's promises of healing and found freedom through Him. This book will walk you through my personal experience of abuse, the immediate and long-term impacts I experienced as a result of it, and how I evolved in my walk with God to reach healing and freedom from all of it.

It will also give you hope for a future that is unlike anything you can imagine right now. You will receive guidance and tools to move forward in your own healing and in your own faith so that you can break the cycle of abuse you were subjected to and finally experience peace.

I hope that at the end of this journey we take together, you recognize that I am not perfect, and I don't have it all figured out. I don't. In fact, the season of my life in which healing and purpose took hold in my life came about when I realized that I didn't have anything figured out. My decision to seek God, ask Him for direction, and do things differently changed my life completely.

For years, I wondered:

Who would I be if I weren't afraid or angry all the time?
Who would I be if people's dominant personalities didn't cause me to go inside and hide?
Who would I be if I could trust people?
Who would I be if none of this had happened to me?

When I realized that God was calling me to share my story with the world, I was terrified. *What will they think? Or worse, what will they say? Will they pity me? Will they look down on me? Will they trust me around their children knowing I have this awful past?* That became my biggest fear.

Because of all I suffered in childhood, I became the biggest protector of children as an adult. I became hyper-aware of my surroundings and hyper-vigilant, watching every move people made around my children. My mind, unable to rest, kept thinking, *Where are my children? Where are the men? Where are their hands?* I was unable to relax in the company of others. There were too many invisible dangers for me to let my guard down, even for a second. It was exhausting. I prayed for purpose; God answered. I simply couldn't ignore the powerful stirring in my soul to do something meaningful for the purpose of helping others heal. When I decided to answer the call God placed on my life, I was terrified, but full of excitement to participate in the will and work of God.

For years, my mother and husband were the only people who knew I had this desire to share my story. I had not worked up the courage to express it to the world. Once you put something out there, there is an expectation to actually move forward in that direction, and I didn't yet have the courage to do that. I put it off as a task I would tackle later in life, perhaps after retirement, or when I completed a PhD. Writing books just seemed like something you did when you were older, wiser, and thoroughly educated. I also knew meditating on the past would be an overwhelming and emotionally demanding process. Recall that I thought I was through the dark tunnel of my childhood and already out on the other side . . . I didn't really feel like taking a look back at what I had been through. But when God called me to it, I knew it was time.

Writing this book required reflection, disclosure, and, ultimately, *surrender.* Deciding to write the story of your life is a tremendously spiritual experience. God was stirring in me a need to bare my soul. What I did not expect was for God to ask me to tell it *all*. There were things I had never said out loud. There were things that surprised even me when I said them. I reflected on what was done to me and the consequences of those actions. Inevitably, I also confronted the things I had done of my own free will as a result of the abuse I suffered, and the consequences of those actions, too. There were moments in which I thought, *Really God? You want me to tell them that too*? I gained so many new insights throughout the process. It was necessary for me to reach a greater awareness of my pain and for me to understand the true source of those feelings so that God could unlock the chains that had bound my heart and mind for over thirty years. He was leading me to this moment all along; I just didn't know it.

In the past year, I experienced miracle after miracle in my life. God showed me His love, mercy, and power in a way I had never experienced before. As I surrendered to His will and revealed to Him my true feelings, He revealed the path to the life He wanted for me. He didn't just show it to me; He walked me through it and gave me the life He desired for me all along. My life, marriage, and parenting are entirely different now than they were before my healing began. I experienced, firsthand, God's healing power. The weight of my past is dissipating, and I am starting to trust and bond authentically with others—something I was unable to do for nearly a lifetime.

I decided to share my journey of healing for many reasons. I want to step into battle and fight the evil that preys on innocent children by exposing it to the light. I want to point you toward the path of healing and give you some tools to make them a reality in your life. Healing and breaking the cycle of abuse begins with *you*.

The amount of violence and abuse that the women in my family lineage experienced is proof that there is a very real spiritual world that affects us, and our salvation is what is ultimately at stake. The women in my family were also victimized by people they loved and trusted. Their story is not mine to tell, but I can share that ours is a generational issue—a cycle that we need to end. I choose to trust God and to ask Him for His healing and comfort for me, my family, and all the girls, women, and mothers who are still in pain and being affected by their past.

You have the power to change the course of your life, your children's lives, and that of future generations. I want you to recognize the power you have within your family and community. Your choices matter: You can embrace that truth and accept the responsibility that comes with it. If you choose to deal with your past and let Him transform you, you will pave a different path for your children and their children. I have seen God's transformative and healing power at work in my life, and I want you to know about it because His promises are available for you as well. He took human form with you and me in mind. He walked the earth and offered himself as a sacrifice for our pain. He wants to cleanse you, heal you, and set you free.

I hope that my journey will inspire you to courageously confront your past wounds, process the pain you have been ignoring, and accept healing from your Creator in the humility that comes from knowing we cannot do it on our own. If you *DESIRE* to heal, *DEPEND* on God to take your pain, and *DECIDE* to live life with Him at your side, He will transform your life, break the cycle of abuse passed on to you by past generations, and ensure that you and your future generations have a more positive story to tell.

Wherever you are in your healing journey—reluctant to begin, eager to start, or already working through some things—I want you to know that you will get there if you are willing to do the necessary work and reach for God.

This book is separated into two parts. Part One will walk you through my journey of abuse and show you the specific areas of my life that were affected and influenced by those painful experiences. You will have an opportunity to examine and reflect as you read and identify areas where you have yet to be set free. While I will not cover all that I have experienced in life, my goal is to focus on the key areas that were a challenge throughout my life—my relationships, my marriage, motherhood, and my career—and where I've experienced growth as a result of my faith.

My invitation to you as you read my story is that you approach it with an open mind and heart, regardless of where you stand in your faith. Whether you are skeptical of your need to follow an invisible God, a believer who continues to struggle with the wounds of your past, or someone who has already arrived at an awareness of how your past continues to affect you but don't know how to get free, this book is for you. Healing is a process, and this book will guide you through if you allow it. God will be there to support you. He loves you. He sees you entirely and wants more than anything to heal your broken heart.

Part Two will walk you through the moments that God used to heal different areas of my life. In this section, I will give you some tools to reach for that you can use for your own healing.

If you are wondering, "Have I healed? How do I know? What does being healed even mean?" This book is for you. Imagine if you could be sure that you have been healed. You, too, can invite Him into the painful places in your heart, receive healing, and watch Him transform your life. This section will also provide you with a better understanding of what it means to walk with God, to seek and hear His voice, and to unlock the promises of God over your life. You can choose to live in His grace as you step into His perfect desires for you.

As you read, you may find yourself triggered as you reflect on your memories. There will be moments when you will feel your feelings surfacing. It's possible you will even experience some dreams as you begin to tackle the scars of your past. I promise you, there is purpose even in your dreams. There were things God worked out in my dreams that I did not have the courage or knowledge to confront in my waking hours. There were also moments in my healing journey that were overwhelmingly painful and exhausting; but after a good cry, I would have a night of the most restful sleep imaginable and would wake up feeling brand new. Time and time again, I revealed my pain, and He released me from it in new and surprising ways.

If you are finding it difficult to get through your emotions alone, seek help. A friend, counselor, pastor, or mentor can be a great partner and shoulder for you to lean on as you move through your own healing journey. I could not have done my healing work alone. My husband was who I turned to when the dialogue in my mind or between me and God needed a human outlet, and we are closer because of it. Don't give up even when things get hard. My prayer is that you will choose to do the challenging work of dealing with your childhood wounds; feel the feelings that come up no matter how painful; invite God into your life and ask Him for guidance; and, ultimately, surrender your abuse to Him, allowing Him to uproot its power over you and set you *free*. Through this process, He will bring you the support that you need now and will need in the future. God wants to give you a life that is beautiful and free of the shame passed down to you by the evil choices of those who harmed you.

Today, I am a new creation, firmly planted in the promises of God's forgiveness and redemption. My journey will shine a light toward the path of healing. If you are willing to embark on this journey, *healing* and *freedom* for all of eternity is the promise that awaits you on the other side. You may have heard the saying, "There is light at the end of the tunnel." I see the journey of healing from abuse precisely like that. You were left in a dark tunnel when darkness entered into your life, and to get out of it, you will have to walk through it. It will be difficult and painful at times, but you will not be going through it alone. God will be holding your hand and walking with you throughout the process. You are not alone, even when it feels like it. The light at the end of the tunnel is the light I want to direct your attention to as I share my story. Imagine the beams of this light as a helping hand, a rope, or a lifeline that is reaching for you. Let that light guide you and give you hope. Reach for it. Grab it and don't ever let it go. If you are unable to see it from where you are today, I pray my journey will encourage you and give you hope for the future. If you decide to walk forward even when it's difficult and push through to the other side, what awaits you is a bright and peaceful future that's worth the journey.

I marvel at all of the beauty and peace in my life now. It's more than I ever imagined, and the opposite of the life I had growing up. I wasn't always the confident and empowered woman I am today. I will be forty years old this year. If you are younger than me, I want to help you come out of the darkness much sooner. If you are older than me, I want to help you finally bring peace into your life through God.

I now know the truth: I am never going to be able to *earn* the gift of forgiveness and salvation. I will continue to struggle and make mistakes. That is true for all of us. We will never reach perfection while we walk this earth—and that's okay; God knew that from the beginning. I don't deserve the amount of grace I received, but such is our God. He loves us exactly as we are. This one realization completely transformed my faith and walk with God. I wish I knew the truth back then—that forgiveness and salvation are a *gift*. We just have to accept salvation to receive it, and choose to walk in that grace, daily.

And one more thing. This journey I've been on of sharing and healing opened the door for others to also share their experiences with me. At times I felt heavy, as though I were carrying the pain of others, and realized that I was relying on myself to hold that pain and do something, and that is not what God called me to do. God calls us to be there for one another but to continue to give it all to Him—*He is the healer.* There truly is nothing I can do for anyone apart from God. So please don't set your sights on me as your beacon of light and hope; I am just a messenger sharing the message God has given me through my life and experiences. Human nature is human nature, and much of how we experience the world around us is wired into us. We process pain in similar ways and respond to our bruises and scars similarly, so there will likely be a lot in my story that you will relate to. We were also created to heal in specific ways, so the roadmap will likely be similar for you and me.

I encourage you to trust God with all your heart as we walk this journey together.

Part One

WHAT HAPPENED AND WHO
I BECAME AS A RESULT

CHAPTER 1

My Story of Abuse

My story begins before I was born. It starts with my mother, who was born into extreme poverty in El Salvador. She was one of six children born to my grandmother: She had a half-brother, three living sisters, and two children had not survived. My grandmother's firstborn son died at the tender age of six months of unknown causes. Another baby girl was stillborn with a major deformity. My grandparents Cecilia and Rafael were poor farmers struggling to feed their children in a mountainous region of the tiny impoverished country of El Salvador. Imagine living without electricity, running water, or even doors and walls that fully covered the interior of your home. When times were good, their small plot of land and door-less hut made of sticks and hay provided enough fruits and vegetables for the family to eat a small meal. During the good times, they harvested corn, beans, squash, and mangos. Most days, the family didn't know where their next meal would come from. When the family had nothing to eat, my mother, a young girl of ten years old, helped the neighboring women with chores, grinding corn for handmade tortillas, washing clothes, and caring for the children. In exchange, she received a small plate of beans and tortillas. Many days, her family depended on that small meal to sustain them. My mother didn't own a pair of shoes. On her way home, she would hide her bare feet behind a rock or bush when she encountered people.

My mother was thirteen years old when my grandfather died. That's when life really got hard. Her father's death left my grandmother a

1

widow with five children to raise on her own. My grandmother became the man and woman of the house. She farmed the small plot of land to feed the family.

At her young age, my mother was already experiencing harassment and sexual advances. My grandfather's firstborn lived with the family. He was the oldest of the five siblings and protected the women from drunks and other men who harassed them daily. Fist to fist he fought off any offender, and managed to protect them for a while. Sadly, he was murdered by his girlfriend's brother only one year after my grandfather passed.

My mother was fourteen years old the first time she left home to work in the city. Many of the local girls her age had already left their families for jobs as maids. A close friend of my mother's secured a job working for a family in Santa Ana, one of the more affluent cities in El Salvador. She offered to refer my mother to a family who could hire her as live-in help, and she did. Optimistic for the prospect of a steady meal and roof over her head, she left home to work for a family in the same neighborhood where her friend worked.

The family my mother worked for was kind. My mother cleaned, washed, and ironed clothes, and made tortillas in return for three meals a day. Being so young, she was afraid of sleeping alone and told her friend she was going back home. Her friend convinced her to stay. Instead, they made an arrangement: She continued to work there but slept with her friend at the other family's house, returning first thing in the morning to begin her work.

The lady of the house had several sons. They were musicians and would return from gigs late and drunk. It wasn't long before one of them entered her room late at night. My mother woke up to someone caressing her hair as she slept in her bed. Terrified, she pretended to sleep. Thankfully, nothing else happened. That was how she met my father.

Fearful of everything at her young age, she went back home the next day to avoid future harassment. After a time, her friend returned and told my mother she was quitting her job with that family. She was engaged to be married and convinced my mom to replace her. "The boys are harmless," she said. "I've never had any problems. They like to joke, that's all." So my mother returned to the city as the maid in my father's home. That was the beginning of the abusive relationship that terrorized our family for years.

My mother was sixteen years old when I was born. My father was twenty-one years old at the time. He was a musician and an alcoholic. I was only three weeks old the first time he beat her. My father was in the habit of bringing home women, prostitutes and conquests after gigs, and on one particular occasion, my mom decided to speak up against the blatant disrespect. He beat her relentlessly to the point where she had to run away in the middle of the night to hide, leaving me behind with an uncle. She hoped he would calm down by the time she returned. He didn't. He attacked her again the minute she walked in the door.

With a newborn in her arms, she fled him for the first time and returned home to her family. However, it didn't take long for her to realize she would not have the means to feed me. She worried I would be malnourished and starve. So she made the choice to return to my father's home, fully aware of the abuse that awaited her.

Around that time, violence in the area was escalating.

"In the year 1980, El Salvador suffered from one of the bloodiest and long-lasting wars which lasted for a twelve-year period. This war caused the deaths of 75,000 people, and many innocent people were separated from their families. A lot of the people killed were innocent children and mothers."[1]

My parents were preparing to leave the country in search of a better life in the United States, but my mom chose to stay and bear the verbal, emotional, and physical abuse that was already dominating her life with my father and join him on the journey. She planned to leave him once they made it to American soil. I was eighteen months old when we arrived in Los Angeles, California. My little brother was born one year

---

[1] Merritt, Maria. "The Civil War of El Salvador." Prezi. 2 February 2016. https://prezi.com/qdqezzt08zwg/the-civil-war-of-el-salvador/

later. My mother worked in a catering truck as a cook. Life was hard as my mother struggled to support the entire family.

Needless to say, my childhood was not the joyful, carefree beginning in life a mother dreams for her children. I don't have many memories of our life together as a family. The few devastating and traumatic memories that I can recall today are images no child should have had to go through. My childhood memories are flashes of the violence, abuse, and neglect that were the foundation on which my tender life was formed. I witnessed my father beating my mother many times. I remember her wearing oversized sunglasses in the daytime and at work to disguise her black-and-blue face. My father would drink every day; then the yelling would begin, and eventually, he would be on top of my mom hitting her.

———————————— Healing Exercise 1.1 ————————————

There are many forms of abuse. I experienced several throughout my youth: physical abuse, witnessing domestic violence, verbal abuse, emotional neglect, and sexual abuse. We rarely experience an isolated type of abuse. My guess is that you, too, have experienced a variety of abuses within your trauma. Perhaps you are aware of some but don't realize that other experiences were also abusive. It is important that we identify and acknowledge our experiences before we can address and heal from them. You may have experienced one or more of the following types of abuse.

In *Mending the Soul: Understanding and Healing Abuse*, Steven Tracy discusses the following types of abuse.

- *Physical abuse* occurs when an adult or caregiver purposefully causes physical harm to a minor. This could be as a form of punishment and usually results from frustration and a lack of self-control by adults, parents, or caregivers.
- *Domestic violence* is physical violence or threats of physical harm used to control a spouse or adult family member. Witnessing

domestic violence is abusive not only to the parent being victimized; it also causes deep emotional wounds to children.

- *Verbal abuse* is a type of emotional abuse in which words are used to harm or manipulate another individual. Words can be deeply damaging to a child's self-esteem.
- *Childhood sexual abuse* is the exploitation of a minor for sexual gratification either through touching, sexually suggestive comments, or exposing a minor to sexual acts by and between adults or teenagers.
- *Physical or emotional neglect* is the failure of a caregiver or parent to provide adequate food, care, protection, attention, and emotional support for a child.
- *Spiritual abuse* is the use of spiritual or religious authority, traditions, or the Bible to dominate, manipulate, or force others to allow unhealthy behaviors.

1. *Think back to conversations you have had with a parent, grandparent, older sibling, or other person who could provide perspective into your family's history. Did your parents or grandparents experience abuse? Recognizing that the abuse you experienced was passed down to you from previous generations will equip you for the tough work of forgiving, which we will discuss later.*

2. *What types of abuse did you experience, and by whom?*

3. *Journal your thoughts.*

NO ONE WAS LISTENING

Growing up, our family dynamic left my brother and I vulnerable to abuse, as we had little supervision during the day. While my mother worked, we played with the neighborhood children in and around our apartment building and even in an abandoned building next door. I was five years old the first time a neighbor sexually abused me. He was the older brother of twin girls I played with at the time. That day, I knocked on their door, hoping the twins could come out to play with me. He lured me into his bedroom and took advantage of my trust and innocence. I don't have a complete memory of what happened. I remember arriving and following instructions in a bedroom. He instructed me to take off my pants. I was embarrassed, so I stepped into the bathroom and came out with my pants around my tiny ankles. Next thing I remember, he was hovering over me saying, "Open your legs wider and just watch TV." Chilly Willy the Penguin was being played for me on a medium-sized box television, over a tall wooden dresser. When I left, he said, "Tell them I was showing you my Atari."

I was six years old the year we escaped my father. The day we left, I had gone to a birthday party with a neighbor. When we returned, my mother's cousin and my aunt's boyfriend were parked outside waiting to take me to my mother. We never returned to that building, and we never lived with my father again.

My mother had found the courage to leave with the help of a neighbor, who became my stepdad overnight. Though we were in hiding, it didn't take long for my father to find us. One day there was a knock on the door, and there he was—my father. He had found us. I remember the look of fear on my mother's face as she treaded lightly around the conversation. My little brother must have been three years old at the time. "We have a new dad," he blurted out. The next thing I knew, my mother was on the sidewalk with my father over her, strangling her. Thank God for the neighbor that interfered that day. He ripped my father off my mom and ushered us all into his apartment. He stood in the doorway and didn't let my dad in.

My father eventually left. He returned days later and snatched my brother, leaving a shoe behind in the middle of the street by accident. Thankfully, he returned my brother later that day. I didn't have the same luck the day my father's brother picked me up from my new school. I was kidnapped for over four months. During that time, I was enrolled in a school in a mostly African American community. I was one of only a handful of Hispanic children, that I knew of. I was bullied and felt completely alone. I was also afraid of my father. He was always drunk and, on one occasion, he picked me up on his lap; when I tried to get away from him, he bit my ear, hurting me and scaring me further. I refused to sleep in his bed that night. Instead I slept with his mother, a bitter woman who despised my mother and was ecstatic to finally be free of us. Back at home, my mother struggled to get me back from my father. She called every night, but my grandmother coached all of my responses when I was given the phone. I was told to tell my mother that I never wanted to go back home, and I did. My mother cried and eventually the phone was snatched out of my hands. I was taken at the beginning of the fall season and was not returned until after the New Year. I received one gift that Christmas, and it wasn't from my father. My uncle's girlfriend gave me a set of play dishes. I watched as everyone around me unwrapped gift after gift, leaving a pile of torn wrapping paper scattered everywhere. My father eventually agreed to allow my mother to visit me after the holidays. One morning, my mother arrived to see me, and, to my surprise, so did Christmas, in a huge plastic bag full of presents: babies, Barbies, clothing, shoes, and a variety of other toys. I ran into her arms, and she cried uncontrollably as she held me tightly. I overheard my parents speaking. She promised she would get back together with him, and based on that promise he allowed me to go home with her. I was always a petite child but, on this occasion, I remember my family marveling at how skinny and pale I had gotten once I returned. I was also infested with lice.

By this time, I had already attended three schools in the beginning months of my first-grade year when we went on the run again. We moved into a small two-bedroom apartment not far from the one we shared with my father. The four of us—my mom, my little brother, my stepfather, and I—shared one bedroom while my mother's cousin, whom we called "Uncle Nathan" rented the other room. We had just escaped my father, and things were getting better, when my mother's cousin began molesting me. He was my favorite uncle—a man I loved and trusted. He gave me gifts, money, and a lot of attention. Somehow, I always ended up on his lap. No one noticed he was fondling me over my clothes. At times, I would wake up in my mother's bed with someone's hand in my underwear. I had learned that even a minor movement of my body would alert him that I was waking up and the fondling would stop. I knew it and used that knowledge to make it stop. I wiggled my small body and the hand would retrieve.

I don't know how or when I learned the word sex. I must have been seven years old the first time I told my cousins, "I've done that before." Puzzled and in disbelief, the boys questioned my statement, to which I firmly answered, "Yes I have. With Nico. He's my boyfriend." Nico was the teenager who molested me when I was five.

The children, neighbors who overnight had become my cousins, told their mother. A short time later, I overheard the grownups talking about it. "Dicen que Nico viola a la Karlita," my new aunt told my stepdad and their mother. "They say Nico raped little Karla," was the statement. There was no response. No one was outraged. I was never approached or questioned on the subject. That summer, we went camping with Nico's family, and I recall yearning for Nico's attention. The neighbor who abused me when I was five had "groomed" me, as had my uncle. Grooming consists of gaining the trust of a child and their parents to get access to and exploit them. With the full confidence of my parents and my own, these men had access to me and took advantage, violating my body, trust, and spirit. At the time, I didn't know what was happening, or why, or that it was wrong.

God designed us for love, we yearn for it, we desire it, we want to give it, and when we receive it, we attach to those who show us kindness. These are all God-given desires, we were created by Love and for love (1 John 4:8). However, when love is given to us in such twisted ways, to manipulate and exploit us—especially at such a tender age—love becomes distorted. We don't realize that what we received was actually evil disguised as love, serving selfish purposes for those who gave it. That yearning planted so much shame in me, and that shame is the reason why I remained silent about the abuse for years. As a child, I blamed myself, I thought I was responsible for it since I kept it a secret. Later, as an adult, I hated myself for caring about the people who abused me; I even questioned if I had enjoyed it.

Another time, in my elementary school cafeteria, kids were talking about sex, and I again said, "I've done that." An aide overheard and loudly said to me, "What did you say?"

I froze.

My friend came to my rescue and said, "She's talking about a movie."

It was clear she did not believe him, but she didn't press further. Nothing else happened.

The lack of response by the adults responsible for my care and safety was one of the most devastating tragedies of my childhood. I didn't recognize this then, but I understand now the reason for the silence of my stepfamily. Recall we were immigrants, here from a foreign country where violence against women was, and continues to be, rampant. El Salvador is recognized still today as "one of the world's most dangerous places to be a woman."[2] In the middle of excruciating poverty and the terror of the civil war that erupted as a result, violence against women simply wasn't something people questioned or reported. It was the sad status quo, and that victimization followed us into this country. Compounding the silence was the fact that, at the time, we were all here illegally—afraid to be deported back to a place where we may not live another day if sent back. I recognize now the quiet plight of immigrant communities who remain silent as a result of fear and a survival instinct; they would rather suffer in silence here than go back to a starving country where their lives are under threat of death daily.

PIECING IT TOGETHER

I remember what happened to me, but not entirely. I do not remember all the details. In some cases, I can see the beginning and the end of a moment or a still image of something inappropriate. What I remember most was feeling dirty, anxious, and confused. What I

---

[2] Donovan, Louise. "Men Kill Women Because They Can: Inside El Salvador's Devastating Femicide Crisis." Elle. 01 April 2019. https://www.elle.com/uk/life-and-culture/a25626891/el-salvador-femicide-crisis/

cannot recall has always been a mystery to me. I've often asked, *God, how far did it go? Please tell me.* Growing up, I wanted to know all that had happened, I used to pray, "God, am I a virgin?" I repeated this prayer too many times to count. I asked God to make a leaf move if I was a virgin; make the next car that goes by a specific color if I was a virgin; make this or that happen if I was a virgin. I begged Him to please give me some sign or show me the full extent of what happened.

That full clarity never came to me. It was hard living in that uncertainty throughout my youth. The memories I do have replay in my mind, interrupting my life in the most inappropriate circumstances, so I know now that God was protecting me. It is as if He shielded the eyes of my mind from seeing the full experience.

CHAPTER 2

Immediate Emotional Impacts

I didn't know it when I was a child, but I developed an ability to fall deep into my own mind and block out the outside world when things were unbearable. When my parents fought, people yelled, or things were happening that were too ugly to bear, I went inside and hid. Chaos was happening all around, but I was safe inside. I could look from afar as if looking at a distant image through a window, hearing only the muffled sound of familiar voices. For a long time, I hated not knowing with certainty all those years how far the violations went. Not being able to recall the full memory left me with many questions, but it also saved me from re-experiencing the abuse in my mind innumerably more times.

The trauma manifested itself through changes in my behavior at home and school. For years I suffered from nightmares and anxiety. The nightmares were unbearable. I was terrified to fall asleep. They would come like clockwork. Recurring dreams terrorized me constantly. In them, I would arrive at school pant-less, naked, or wearing only one shoe. Realizing it, I would run in search for a place to hide. I never seemed to find refuge anywhere. Then there was the quicksand. In this particular scenario, I would get chased by a monster I couldn't see. Climbing onto a tree in despair, I realized what lay below was quicksand. I became tired, slipped, and began sinking.

I also had night terrors. On one occasion, I woke up from a nightmare and ran to my mother asking for help. I could see a large red horse in my room trying to trample me. The beast filled the small room my brother and I shared with my mother and stepfather. My mother frantically tried to calm my panic. I began to hit her. I was horrified.

Then there was the tickling and falling that felt so real! I would jump out of my slumber fearing someone was tickling me in my sleep. I could feel the fingers jabbing into my ribs relentlessly! After falling I would bounce inches above my bed and awaken with a jolt.

In my nightmares, I would attempt to cry out for help, hoping someone would wake me, but the sound never left my body. I wasn't even safe in my sleep! It was torture.

I was afraid of everything and didn't trust anyone. I was anxious and fearful *all the time*. I can only describe the feeling in my dreams and even during my waking hours as being mangled in a car wreck: metal crushing and piercing my skin, my body distorted and trapped. I have never experienced a car accident to recognize what that might feel like, but this is how I imagined metal crushing and piercing through my body would feel. That's what my days and nights felt like. I overheard adults saying I was having some sort of psychological issue. No one ever asked me what was happening to me, but I assume they attributed it all to the very ugly divorce and custody battle between my parents.

As a child, I was taught to respect and listen to adults. I was taught to not talk back, and disagreement of any kind was seen as disrespectful in my home. I was often hit for speaking my mind. Men often called my mother on the phone. I was jealous for my mother's attention and protective of our family, so I told my stepfather when he got home one night. My parents went into the bedroom and had a fight. When my mother left the room, she walked toward me with anger in her eyes and determination in her steps. She slapped me squarely across my cheek, knocking me off the armrest of the sofa where I had been attentively listening to the shouting emanating from the room. It was at this point I lost my power, my voice, and trust in the adults around me. As a result, going forward, I stayed silent in moments when I should have said something. I did not have the knowledge or self-confidence to respond to what was happening to me. I did not trust my mother and stepfather, so I stayed silent.

I was angry. The violent fights I began having with my little brother were a matter of concern. My grandmother used to say I would one day kill him. Hearing these hurtful statements only made me feel more damaged and unworthy. I also began lying. I once told my fourth-grade teacher that a man was following me at school, that he parked his van outside the school gates and watched the children. School police were called, and when asked about the details and what color the van was, I told them it was a different color every day. At that moment, I knew by the look in the detective's eyes that he did not believe me. The investigation was dropped. No one ever asked me directly if anyone was hurting me.

CHAPTER 3

A Dawn Starts to Break

When I was eight years old, my mom would take me to work with her on school vacation breaks. Her boss was a Christian man whom she had confided in about the issues I was having—my nightmares, aggression, and lying. On one of my trips to her work, my mother's boss asked me if I knew of Jesus. I did not. He told me, "Jesus is the son of God, and He wants to help you." He said, "He came to save us. If you accept Jesus as your Lord and Savior, He will enter your heart and live with you forever."

That afternoon on the metal floor of that catering truck, I knelt before the son of God and repeated a prayer accepting Him into my life. I would never be alone again.

That was when everything began to change in my life. Life has been getting better and better ever since. My problems didn't end overnight, but there was a definite shift in my life after that moment. I found comfort in knowing that God was with me.

I began attending a small Church with my grandmother and my aunts. I quickly learned I loved to sing worship to God because of the sense of peace and majesty I felt within those moments. I felt connected to God and enjoyed learning about heaven.

Everything I knew about what it meant to be a Christian I learned in our tiny church from our pastor and my aunts. I don't remember at which point this list of unspoken rules materialized for me, or how it was delivered, but the list of rules we followed included for the women: no makeup, jewelry, pants, or short skirts. Generally, we (Christians) were also not to participate in "worldly activities," such as listening to music other than to worship God. We could not dance, and alcohol was strictly forbidden for all. My parents did not attend church or live by any of these standards, and because these standards weren't lived out within my home, our home life always tripped me up.

Our church focused a lot on the book of Revelation, and often the message was one that stirred fear and dread. We were taught that Jesus would return one day for His Church, and we needed to remain faithful in order to be saved from the scary end of civilization. I will forever remember the night our admired pastor picked up a charm I wore on a gold necklace around my neck, looked into my eyes and said, "You shouldn't wear this. You wouldn't want Jesus to find you wearing it when He comes to take His people." These two sentences, while well intended, had a deep and destructive impact on my childlike faith and walk with God.

It scared me to think that if I did something wrong, Jesus might leave me behind. I didn't recognize it initially, but what it created was an incorrect concept of the nature of God. I learned that God was inflexible; He was a strict and punishing God. After that, I thought it was so easy to lose our salvation and so difficult to obtain it. For the majority of my youth, I attended church with extended family. My parents attended church for a brief period. As a family, we attended a small church in downtown Los Angeles, where I met the man who would one day become my husband.

I understood early on that salvation was an individual choice, and our relationship with God could not be passed down to us—it was something that needed to be born in our heart and pursued by us genuinely. Nonetheless, our families do influence us. For the most part, Christianity was not modeled, taught, or supported in my home. I often found myself at family gatherings where secular music was being played, and my family enjoyed dancing. In fact, it was something that the whole family enjoyed in celebrations. It didn't matter that we were all crowded into the small living room of someone's apartment, people were dancing and the children were no exception. All, from young to old, grabbed partners and joyfully "shook our tails."

This was hard for me. On one hand, I wanted to serve God and make it to the pearly gates of heaven. On the other, I was taught that dancing was a sin, and I felt like a complete outsider in my own family. I would sit out on the sidelines while everyone else delighted in twirling and spinning joyfully with one another. I would eventually give in to twirling with the other children too. In the back of my mind, my heart would sink, and I couldn't fully enjoy myself because I knew that, once again, I had lost my ticket into heaven. I tried so hard to abstain from breaking all the rules I had learned in church, but often I was unable to "resist temptation." I felt like a failure, as though no matter how hard I tried, I would never be able to measure up and earn my place in heaven. I didn't give up and, despite coming to know God as a forgiving God, I never felt good enough. I felt I kept messing up.

I chose to be baptized just before my fifteenth birthday. By then, I had begun to volunteer at church, initially helping to care for the little ones. I would watch them in a tiny room in the back of the small storefront that was our church home. After I was baptized, I was able to take on some leadership roles within our small congregation and even got to lead worship service more than once. I also began teaching Sunday school to the little children, and eventually I was even asked to deliver a message. I was fourteen years old the first time I stood before the congregation and delivered a message that must have lasted all of ten or fifteen minutes. I don't know what I chose to teach on that night—what I remember most were my nerves. I read the verses I had studied, said a few words, and then pretty much went blank. The pastor rescued me and finished the message. The night I led worship, I had a short list of familiar songs, which I sang with our tiny congregation, and I enjoyed it very much.

Our church was tiny—at most we had thirty members attending services almost every night. The comfortable family atmosphere and closeness to God were what kept me coming back. That time in worship and closeness to God sustained my faith for many years, even if it was an on-and-off relationship of sorts.

My dreams changed during this time, too. I began having a new recurring dream. In it, I was flying through the sky, soaring over beautiful mountains or the city buildings. I interpreted my dreams as indicators of what was happening in my life and the closeness with God I was developing. A nightmare would begin and, in my slumber, I remembered I could pray the name Jesus and interrupt the dream. Other times, I simply flew away from the situation. This was a marked shift in my life. I had someone I could turn to when I needed it, even when no one else seemed to be listening. He was there ready to help when I called on Him. I didn't know it then, but He was there, always working behind the scenes to rescue me from the life I was born into.

CHAPTER 4

Darkness Revealed

B y this point, we had been living with my stepdad for a few years, and my father had moved on. He was living with the lovely woman who remains his wife today. He was no longer hunting us. Eventually, we moved to another apartment in the same building with just one room, and my uncle no longer lived with us—but the abuse continued. He began making sexually suggestive comments. I still remember the day he called, and I picked up the phone, only to have him ask me, "Do you want to have sex with me?" I was nine years old. By then, I had already stumbled across a pornographic magazine in one of our closets, and having been beaten for looking at it, I had pieced together that sex was a very bad thing. I was startled by the question and hung up on him. The next time he came to visit, he asked why I had hung up on him. I told him my mom had walked in the room. Thankfully, he never asked the question again.

After we left my father, my mother began hitting us, and I was afraid of her. I also felt responsible for the abuse. I had followed directions and kept silent. I thought I would get in trouble for having let him touch me.

I was ten years old and in the fifth grade when I received health education, or "sex ed" as we called it. It was the first and only time an adult had ever had a conversation with me about my body and puberty. It was then I realized that what was happening to me was indeed wrong. It gave me the strength to see the abuse for what it was: a crime against a child. Around the same time, the Drug Abuse Resistance Education, commonly known as D.A.R.E. To Say No campaign, was in full effect at our school. This program, while aimed at drug abuse prevention, gave me the knowledge and strength to finally say NO and put a stop to my uncle's abuse.

This knowledge gave me the confidence to confront my uncle. I finally had the words. I convinced my step-cousin that we were both in danger and needed to make it stop. A bit confused and hesitant, she agreed to stand by my side as I confronted him. I told him, "I don't like the way you touch us, and if you don't stop, I am going to tell the police." He was shocked. Later, he asked me why I had said those things. He told me I should never say those things around other people again because someone might believe it, and he could get in a lot of trouble. It never happened again.

I didn't fully understand it yet, but I can see now that God was bringing the right people around me to guide and support me. Fifth grade was a pivotal year for me, and my teacher, Mrs. Cantwell, was like an angel sent from heaven. She stepped in to build a support system around me. Seeing the dynamics in my family, she placed me in an Alateen support group, a program for kids affected by someone else's drinking. School became my safe place and that group of kids my second family. She and the school psychologist who led the group, and those kids, provided support at a time when I desperately needed it. It was within that safe space that I spoke up about the abuse for the first time.

One of my friends in the group told me a man had recently exposed himself and chased her around the stairwells of her apartment building. I encouraged her to tell the group. In my mind, I was already planning to tell the group what had happened to me, if she was brave enough to share her story. She did, and when she told the group as planned, I did too. I cried uncontrollably as she went into what happened to her, knowing that I too was going to speak up that day.

At the time, I only felt safe enough to tell the group about the time I was abused by my neighbor when I was five years old. I didn't have the courage to tell them about my uncle because that had only stopped recently and he was family. I told them a sanitized version of the incident with the neighbor that made me feel less responsible and less powerless. I told them I had fought him and ran away. I was given an opportunity to have a conversation with my mother before the school called her in to discuss the matter with her, and I did. I told her the same version, leaving out the true details, and never mentioning what happened with my uncle, who was still very close to my mom and very much a part of our lives. The abuse I had experienced with my uncle remained my shameful secret for years.

Although I hadn't told the whole story, I was free enough in that group to start to open up. I was free to be myself, and I could express my feelings without fearing physical punishment. I was among a group of people who loved me without judgement because we were all experiencing similar pain.

I will be eternally grateful for these wonderful in-school programs. The "sexual education" I received, at a time when no one else was talking to me about sex in an accurate and safe environment, was instrumental to enlightening me about appropriate and inappropriate physical interaction. The D.A.R.E. program gave me the words and courage to say no to harmful and dangerous things and finally put a stop to the abuse I experienced at the hands of my uncle for years. The support group provided a safe, nonjudgmental, and supportive environment where I could open up about the pain I was in and also provided validation by confirming that those experiences were inappropriate and hurtful.

These resources did wonders for my self-esteem and well-being. I found my voice, self-confidence, and belonging among the small group of friends I had found amidst it all. I was even chosen to give the commencement speech at our sixth-grade graduation.

We were created in the image of God by the Creator of the universe. With His words, He spoke the world into existence, and breathed life into all of it, and all of us (Genesis 1:3). Therefore, God's power is within us, and our words have the capacity to build as well. Our voices were given to us as a method for expressing, connecting, creating, and protecting.

My voice was silenced for a time but never destroyed, and in this season, it was my voice that finally saved me from continuing to be a victim of my uncle. It was with my voice that I accepted Jesus into my heart when He approached me, through the voice of my mother's boss. I didn't recognize this even then, but my voice carried so much weight and power.

Your voice is powerful, and with it you can also change the course of your life. Speaking out your experiences will help you to release the pain and tension of the secrets hidden within you. I encourage you to find a group of women with similar life experiences, so you can openly talk through the hurtful things you experienced.

CHAPTER 5

The Residue of Abuse

A fter the Northridge earthquake in 1994, a magnitude 6.7 earthquake that struck in the San Fernando Valley area of Los Angeles, fear tightened its grip on my life. The epicenter was only a few miles from our home in Sun Valley and shook our two-story townhome dramatically. For the first time, my brother and I shared a room separate from our mother and stepfather. We were sleeping at 4:30 in the morning when the earthquake struck. The aftershocks were pretty strong and were felt for days. While our home suffered minimal structural damage, the emotional shock I experienced was severe. After the earthquake, we slept in our backyard for weeks, eventually moving into our living room, and finally back upstairs into our bedrooms. I began having trouble sleeping again. I was terrified to fall asleep. I would go into a panic every night. My mom slept in my bed with me for months. At one point, I was even prescribed sleeping pills because I could not fall asleep or stay asleep.

Sun Valley is known for high incidents of respiratory diseases due to the poor air quality and proximity to a nearby waste management site. I became physically ill with pneumonia, hay fever, and asthma as a result of sleeping outside. I was prescribed breathing treatments around the clock, and I didn't go to school for months. My grades began to decline at that point. I had once shown a lot of promise. I had been outgoing and outspoken, but then totally went inside. The abuse had stopped, but I became a quiet teenager who hid in my room most of the time. I was afraid of men, boys, and life.

When I was fifteen years old, our youth pastor, who was at the time 24 years old, became interested in me. He began calling me on the phone and started giving me more personal attention than the other youth in our group. I enjoyed it. It made me feel unique that such a smart and godly man was interested in me. One day on one of our long conversations over the phone, he asked me to run away with him to El Salvador. Thankfully, I had recently visited our country and seen the extreme devastation and poverty in the country. While I was there, men made sexually suggestive comments to me everywhere I went, which scared me. I knew instantly that was not the life I wanted. I ended the friendship immediately, and my mom no longer allowed me to go to church. I had really enjoyed the friendship, mentorship, and safety I felt at church up until that point. I found myself once again feeling alone and afraid.

Our early life experiences cling to us.

As I continued to grow up, I played it safe, kept my guard up, avoided conflict, worked hard to please people, and showed my frustrations only at home with the people closest to me. At home I worked hard to please my mother by cleaning and caring for my siblings. By now my mother and stepfather had married, and my little brother and sister had been born. I remained a docile and timid child at school and church but exploded in anger at home and continued to have violent fights with my brother. As he got older, my brother spoke to me harshly, in the same manner we had seen my father treat my mother, and I responded the only way I knew to respond to conflict: by hitting. I once slapped him for calling me a bitch, only to have my mother return the aggression back to me by slapping me in front of him for what I had done. This only encouraged him, while reminding me that what I needed to do was be silent and take it. This, however, was nearly impossible, as a fight had been born in me and I was unable to silence it. I was constantly in a fight with my brother, mother, and stepfather for speaking my mind. It was a tense and stressful environment I couldn't wait to break out of.

That was how I began to walk through life—able to function outside but lashing out at home. I succeeded for years at this dual demonstration. To the world, I was confident, smart, and well put together. At home, I was sweet and loving but exploded with anger and rage I couldn't control when things got hard. It was as though I had split myself in two.

I spent the next decade trying to figure out who I was in light of the abuse I had experienced, who God was and who He wanted me to be, and trying to navigate life. I didn't know how to express my feelings in a healthy way. I became very skilled at pushing pain "under the rug." There it remained hidden and unresolved for years.

I became timid and reserved. At this point, girls and boys were beginning to date or like each other. I began to like boys but was terrified of them and of my feelings for them. I did not want to go back to that prison of shame that caved in on me when I was touched. I went through junior high and high school quietly, enjoying friendships and school. Even with the pain I was still holding inside, I always liked school and felt safe—as long as I avoided boys. I never felt safe around boys or men, or alone.

SEXUAL CONFUSION

One of the biggest impacts from abuse was that I was very confused about sexuality, and from a young age. When I was a child, I began playing touching games with other children. I played "boyfriend and girlfriend" games that involved kissing or touching them over their clothes in the same way I was touched by my uncle. I was eight years old the first time I kissed a girl in a closet. She was slightly younger than I, and I could tell this shocked her and she didn't enjoy it. I can see now how normal her reaction was, but at the time, I remember being confused by it. When I was around twelve years old, I also played these games with another friend. One night, she came to my house for a sleepover, and, while everyone slept, she and I played a game that involved me kissing her body. While I was afraid of boys and didn't trust them, I felt comfortable with and unthreatened by girls. I also didn't mind taking the lead with her in the secret games we played—I initiated them. At the time, I didn't feel ashamed. I didn't know that it was wrong because someone I had loved and trusted had played those games with me. I can't say with certainty if I mistakenly thought this was just the way people interacted with each other or if something else was driving these desires within me. The abuse I had experienced created so much confusion in my mind about what was good and bad, appropriate and inappropriate. One thing is for certain: My sense of right and wrong was compromised.

Puberty was a difficult and confusing time for me. I'm sure it is for all of us. I was introduced to sexuality far before I had the knowledge, maturity, or authority to choose to participate in it. Having been introduced to sexuality at such a young age created a completely skewed perspective for me in which everything was tied to sex. During that age when most of us begin to discover our hormones, I ran in the opposite direction of everything to do with sexuality. I was in junior high when another girl my age made it clear she liked me, and not just in a friendly way. She had become jealous over my friendship with another girl in our group. I didn't understand it. It seemed everyone but me knew that she liked girls. I shied away and steered clear of her friendship; I wasn't prepared to date, nor did I want to, even though other kids my age were already openly dating. Unsure of where I stood with my virginity (my memories still weren't clear), I spent a lot of time thinking about whether I was or wasn't a virgin. These experiences eventually led me to question whether I was or wasn't straight. By this time my mother had begun saying things like, "You have to save yourself for marriage." In my mind, that ship had sailed, which made me feel guilty over the things that Nico and my uncle had done to me.

I was terrified of boys and the men who harassed me and made comments about my body. When my stepfather told people I was "born on a wooden board" because I had nothing in the front and nothing in the back, I knew he was talking about the lack of curves apparent in my body and saw it as confirmation that my value was tied to my body. I never dated, although I did have crushes on boys.

I had my first real boy-crush at age sixteen. He was Salvadoran like me, smart, quiet, and a good friend. I told him I had never been kissed on the lips, and he made it his mission to be the first to kiss me. That was usually the response I got from boys when I made that statement, but this time I wanted to experience that first tender kiss: the kind you see in movies when sparks fly and a perfect romance begins. One afternoon in the quad after school had ended, we sat facing each other. He told me to close my eyes. I felt comfortable and liked him so I did, and he proceeded to kiss me gently on my forehead, then each of my eyelids, cheeks, chin, and eventually my lips. It was the sweetest thing I had ever experienced. I knew then I was ready to date. I wanted that intimacy and protection I felt in his presence. I wanted him to become my first boyfriend, but his mother did not allow him. In fact, he stopped talking to me overnight, which was devastating to me. I found out later that his mother had beat him badly for staying late with me that day and said she would disown him if he dated me. I never understood why his mother didn't feel I was good enough for her son. That was my introduction to dating.

I had my first actual boyfriend soon after at age seventeen. Our romance began just weeks before high school graduation. He was six-foot-three and a star football and basketball player who sweet-talked me into thinking he cared about me. At a graduation party, he made the bold move of placing my hand inside his pants while we were dancing. He was aroused and wanted me to know it. I panicked and left the party. I continued to talk to him on the phone but avoided being alone with him and eventually broke up with him altogether. I had another boyfriend who also attempted to shift the relationship to sex quickly, and once again I ran away and broke up with him over the phone. I desperately desired to be loved and cherished, but each time it became clear that sex had to be a part of the relationship and I fled. Being touched in a sexual way immediately brought on the memories, fear, and confusion that had always been my default state of being. I struggled with flashbacks every time I was held by a man. This made it impossible to move forward physically with the men I dated, in the way they desired. Plus, my faith called me to live in purity, and that meant saving my body in every way for the man I would one day marry.

TURNING AWAY

Then it all changed. After I graduated high school and started my college years at California State University, Northridge (CSUN), I purchased my own car and felt free to do what I pleased. I no longer needed to rely on my parents or the bus for transportation. My first two years at CSUN were hard, but I enjoyed being a student. Learning took me to places I had never experienced or even knew existed. The love of learning is one of the greatest gifts God has given me. Learning is the key to so much in this world: knowledge, access, opportunity, and belonging. Education changed my life, but it wasn't without struggle. Once I had my first full-time job, that became the priority, and I ended up dropping out of school. I also made a conscious choice to leave the Church.

As I got older, the coping mechanism that saved me during the dark years later betrayed me. When I started college, I began to notice a pattern in my focus and an inability to pay attention. When things were hard or overwhelming, I tended to stop listening. If I didn't want to be there, I would just check out. As much as I had loved school, I had a tough time learning once classes became more challenging because I couldn't pay attention.

Staying present and focused became challenging in social situations as well. I would be in the middle of a conversation and suddenly realize I had not been paying attention and didn't know for how long. I'd check back in and think, *How much did I miss?* or *What are they talking about?* I wondered if they knew I hadn't been paying attention. You can imagine how hard it is to form relationships when you can't listen long enough to make a meaningful connection with others. This inability to be present affected my relationships profoundly. I believe this is the main reason I dropped out of school after my first year of college. Sure, there were other reasons—financial concerns, the distraction of boys, and a car that gave me freedom and access to the whole world—but this certainly greatly contributed to my decision to leave.

I used to think daydreaming was harmless until I realized I was hiding. We all get distracted by a random thought from time to time.

We stop paying attention, and our minds wander for a moment. Eventually, something happens and invites us back to the present. This wandering of our minds can be harmless, even healthy. Dr. Leaf, a leading neuroscientist specializing on the mind and brain connection, refers to these moments as "thinker moments" or "awake resting states." Our minds naturally wander; thoughts can surface without invitation; as our brain explores them, we disconnect from the present momentarily. This is a natural process of the brain that occurs when we are thinking deeply. Dr. Leaf asserts, "Research . . . shows that 94 percent of people examined across six continents experience unwanted, intrusive thoughts, images and/or impulses." She goes on to say, "It's not the unwanted, intrusive thoughts that are the problem, but the way they are managed." They only become harmful when we do not manage them.[3] For example, when a negative thought from our past abuse surfaces, we may allow that thought to take over, unmanaged, allowing it to affect our mood and eventually our responses to the outside world in the present. In my case, these moments were a coping mechanism I used to avoid the real world. My daydreaming went on for extended periods. I was thinking of negative experiences, sometimes recent ones or from my past, and entertaining the negative dialogue in my head for far too long—allowing it to affect me in the present. It never occurred to me that I could control my thoughts, that I had the power to reject them or reframe them by creating a more positive internal dialogue. Dr. Leaf asserts that we can and indeed *should* capture every thought, examine it, and choose to shift it into a more positive thought (not a different thought). For example, when these thoughts constantly intruded in my life and relationships, rather than allowing them to replay over and over, I would choose to reject them and shift my thinking by saying something like, "That was an awful thing that happened to me then, but I am not a child anymore and I can choose to set up and maintain strong boundaries to protect myself today."

I had spent many years walking in an incorrect perspective of Christianity. Without the proper guidance, I had done the best I could

---

[3] Leaf, Dr. Caroline. *Think Learn Succeed*, 2018, and *Switch on Your Brain*, 2015.

to learn from those I saw around me. Ultimately, I never felt good enough and, in this season of my life, I gave up on God. There was a moment, when I turned nineteen years old, that I made a decision to walk away.

At the time, I had been attending a campus ministry at CSUN that focused on teaching young Christians how to walk with God. It was what I needed all those years, but having done it on my own without any instruction or accountability all those years, I didn't like it and didn't really understand it. Plus, this ministry placed a lot of boundaries on dating. It was expected that we would go out on group dates. Each Sunday, someone new, who I had absolutely no interest in, asked me out on a "group date." This made me uncomfortable. I didn't feel safe going out with men I didn't know, not even within a church group. There was someone I was interested in getting to know, but dating in the church came with so many rules. We weren't permitted to date by ourselves, we had to go out on double dates or in groups, and there was a great deal of counseling involved. They made it clear that we needed to be sure we were ready for the commitment and responsibility that came with being joined to another as a couple and emphasized the importance of protecting each other by remaining pure and avoiding isolated situations. My mother also opposed me attending this church. She didn't like the amount of time I was spending with church friends and knew I was considering moving out with some of these girls. My friends felt I would benefit from being in a different environment than the family life they knew I had. My stepfather was drinking daily, and our fights were getting worse. My mom was adamantly opposed to me leaving the house to live with these girls.

I was struggling in school and having a tough time adapting and learning to truly walk with God, so I made the decision to walk away. I decided I wanted to live life on my own terms. One day, I made the bold statement within our small Bible study group that I was leaving the Church: "I've decided to live a normal life."

Our words are powerful. The Bible says that what we confess with our mouths has the power to save our lives or destroy us (Proverbs 18:21). Those words marked the beginning of another dark, painful season in my life in which I gave myself over to my desires. I was tired of feeling like a failure and felt that life away from this constant struggle to be perfect would be a better option. My priority became finding a boyfriend, and I was ready to "live my life."

I was nineteen the first time I thought I was actually in love. It didn't go anywhere because I was terrified to be alone with him. The one time I visited him at his dorm, I took my little brother with me to ensure nothing physical would take place. I told him I was a virgin—even though I was never sure. I chose to live as if I were because I had never willingly made the choice to have sex with anyone. Up until that point, I had been determined to save myself for marriage. I knew guys expected access to my body instantly, so I made sure I didn't allow myself to be in places and environments that could lead to engaging in any physical activity. This particular guy said he admired and respected me for it, but the relationship didn't go anywhere; instead, he avoided me. His rejection broke my heart. I cared about him deeply. I began to feel as though the only way a man would ever want me was if I allowed him access to my body.

Just before my twentieth birthday, I met a man a few years older than me. He said and did all the right things to make me feel safe and as though I were in control. Before long, I was convinced I was in love and that he would be my protector. *Finally, a real boyfriend,* I thought. I knew he would want to sleep with me soon after, and I decided when the time came, I was going to do it. I was not going to lose another guy to my past abuse. By that time, I had forgotten that I didn't even know if I was a virgin or not, but I felt I was ready to consciously make the choice to enter into an intimate relationship with a man. He was charming at the beginning. He convinced me that he loved me and after just three months, I slept with him. Then something in him switched; he became possessive, aggressive, extremely jealous, controlling, and outright scary.

I was at school unable to answer his phone calls one afternoon, and he left me an extremely offensive and disrespectful derogatory message. He wiped the floor with what I had given him, and called me every insulting name in the book. He recorded on the message several songs that included demeaning and abusive lyrics toward women. I was disgusted and scared, yet I felt bonded to him because of what I had done and felt I had to make the relationship work. I stayed with him for several months. The relationship went much like that for the duration of the time we were together. I knew that if I stayed with him, I would wind up in an abusive relationship; I already was and didn't even know it.

I finally broke up with him after about eight months. Once I opened that door, there was no turning back. I knew what men expected and concluded it was a normal and expected part of dating relationships. I began to believe it wasn't wrong to sleep with men as long as they were my "boyfriend." My relationships with men were chaotic and on-and-off—not nearly as aggressive as the first—but ultimately, I gave them various degrees of access to my body way too soon and, each time, it became clear that what they were truly after was my body.

I never really spent any time being single after that. I had learned when I was young, incorrectly, that my value was tied to my body, and my experiences with men all seemed to reinforce that relationships with people are tied to sex. I had an inappropriate association in my mind between affection and sexual touching. As a result, once I decided that I *did* want a boyfriend, I slept with every boyfriend I had going forward.

I got myself into a pattern: I was attracted to aggressive, emotionally abusive men who did not respect me, and I would run away not long after, only to move on to my next boyfriend and dysfunctional relationship. It was exhausting and painful.

My standards were low—I was desperate for affection, companionship, and validation. The attention I received from men became the source of my self-worth, and I needed it to feel good about myself. I had low self-confidence and self-esteem, so when men showed me attention and a little bit of affection, I immediately thought I was in love. If they asked me to be their girlfriend, I gave them everything.

SEXUAL REBELLION ——————————————————

In my season of rebellion, I was promiscuous and became addicted to same-sex pornography. While in college, I had access to a computer lab. Many of them were infected with digital viruses that caused floods of pop-ups with pornographic images covering the screen. That is how I first became tempted and ultimately began to watch pornography in secret. At the time, I was still sexually inexperienced and quickly recognized that I didn't enjoy seeing men's naked bodies. It became clear that I was more attracted visually to women, and I began to wonder if I was bisexual. My curiosity grew to the point I began joking with girlfriends about acting out sexually with one another. I began considering the beauty, gentleness, softness, and emotional capacity of women as an alternative to the aggression, disrespect, and fear that surrounded my relationships with men. I began going to gay clubs and considered having a relationship with a woman.

Eventually, what existed only in my mind when I was alone in secret became a desire to experiment with women. I began experimenting sexually with women, and enjoyed it, but doubted that they could give me the protection I desired and fulfill me emotionally. I was at a crossroads, and I knew it.

I continued to notice slightly masculine, yet petite, women and felt attracted to them but ultimately felt most comfortable within a heterosexual relationship, despite the dysfunction that characterized my male relationships. Today, I am satisfied with the instruction left to us in 2 Corinthians 10:5, which tells us to "demolish arguments and every pretension that sets itself up against the knowledge of God," and that we are to "take captive every thought to make it obedient to Christ." I know this isn't a popular point of view in this day and age, but God tells us homosexual attraction goes against His design of sexuality; therefore, I decided to take captive those thoughts and make them obedient to Christ. For me, it was a matter of choice.

CHAPTER 6

Marriage: The Past Resurfaces

C hildhood abuse has profound and long-lasting effects that manifest in subtle and devastating ways in our lives. Unless we are aware of them and do something about them, they remain a part of us, wreaking havoc. Years of abuse caused me to become distrustful of everyone and to fear men. Learning to trust my husband was hard. We were both young and immature when we met, and our relationship triggered all of my fears.

When I was sixteen, I had prayed for my husband. I asked God to prepare a man for me who loves Him above all else. I also asked for him to be tall, dark, and handsome. My husband is the man of my prayers. We started on this journey eighteen years ago.

One evening, as I prepared for my daily run, I received a phone call from a college friend. She excitedly announced: "I have a friend who wants to meet you. He's Salvadoran, like you."

Now, this wasn't the first time this thoughtful friend tried pairing me up with one of her friends, so I didn't respond with the enthusiasm with which she approached it.

But before I could say much else, I was on the phone with Gary. Over the next week, we spent most of our free time talking on the phone until we fell asleep. We shared our backgrounds and discovered we had both lived in the heart of Los Angeles during our childhood and ended up in the San Fernando Valley. Somewhere along the line, the conversation turned to faith, and he shared with me that he was a Christian, and I told him I was too. We began to talk about the churches we each attended as children and soon found out that when I was eight and he was eleven, we had been members of the same church. We came to discover that our parents remembered each other.

We set up a date to meet over dinner and a movie. On my way to meet him, I prayed, "Please God, let him be cute because I'm going to be devastated if he is not." You can see where my priorities were in that season of my life! The truth is, I already loved him and desperately wanted him to be "the one." In fact, just a few months earlier, I had said to God I wanted the next man I dated to be the last. I had been through enough heartache, so I thought. I was ready for happily ever after.

On our first date, he invited me to his apartment and said, "We could watch a movie or we could make a movie." I knew exactly what he meant. He was telling me we would have sex that night, and we did.

We drove to Blockbuster to rent a movie and picked up some takeout to take back to his apartment. His roommate called at one point, and he responded, "Oh, I'm just here hanging out with my new girlfriend." That's all I needed to hear, and I was hooked; I wanted so desperately to be loved. At the end of the movie, we began making out on his couch, and he asked me back to his room. I naively thought we would just make out some more. He undressed me quickly. I said no, but he pressed on, so I gave in.

God, how did I get there so quickly? I was twenty-one by this time, and there had already been four, but this time, I mean . . . I didn't make him work for it at all.

We were dating for exactly one week when he disclosed on a Labor Day morning in front of all his friends that I was going to be the mother of his children. You see, he also had put in his petition to God for the beautiful, Christian, Salvadoran woman that would become his wife. God answered our prayers when He brought us together. Little did we know, we would have to evolve into the people He had prepared us to be for each other.

When two people come together, the beginning is always bliss. The newness of a new relationship is quite possibly one of the sweetest moments we experience in life. Unfortunately, these moments are deceiving and short-lived, and they wear off pretty quickly, leaving us in a world where we put ourselves first and seek to be fulfilled and satisfied by others. This short-term emotion is insufficient to sustain a long-term relationship. That requires so much more.

Our bliss lasted precisely one whole month. It was a cozy October morning, and I woke up in his apartment, me in his pajamas, and he in baggy basketball shorts. I was in the kitchen making him eggs, then set the table for our breakfast when the phone rang. He answered the phone. The one-sided conversation I heard went like this:

"What's up?"

"Uh-huh."

"No, I'm busy."

"Okay."

"Later."

"Who was that?" I asked when he got off the phone.

"No one of any importance," he responded.

I excused myself to the bedroom for a moment and dialed *69 from his bedroom phone. If you grew up in the nineties, you may recognize *69 as the telephone feature that dials back the last incoming call. A woman picked up the phone. I asked who she was, and she proceeded to tell me that she had left her cell phone there the prior weekend. In that instant, the blood flushed clear down to my feet, and my heart crumbled. I recalled that I was unable to reach him the previous weekend. Boldly and clearly, I asked, "Did you sleep with him?"

"Yes."

That was the beginning of the painful on-and-off nature of our relationship. He begged me to forgive him. He said it would never happen again. He assured me he was adjusting to being in a committed relationship. I yelled, cried and left. I eventually came back, and we were hot and cold for the next year.

Around that time, his lease was up, and he was going to need a new roommate. Things were unbearable at home with my parents, mostly because I was staying out all hours of the night and spending the night at his apartment whenever I felt like it. One night, my mother beat me with a belt for the last time. She whipped me to the point of bruising me and accidentally cut me with the buckle. I couldn't wait to get out of that house.

He resisted, but I insisted. We moved in together, and things only got worse. I didn't trust him, and he was drinking way too much for my comfort. The few memories I have of my parents before they divorced were of my father beating my mother in a drunken rage. I swore I would not have that life. I would not tolerate a man who cheated or was an alcoholic. I had already lived that life as a child and refused to pass it on to my future children. For that reason, our relationship continued to be full of anger, fear, and heartbreak. I grew exhausted of playing the spy, going through his things, monitoring his cell phone activity while he slept, and wondering all the time where he was, how much he was drinking, and if he was cheating on me again.

We lived together for about one year, but I could not silence my doubt and jealousy. He drank to the point of becoming belligerent and offensive, often. I was terrified, still angry over his past infidelities, and could not be at peace. When he wasn't home, I wondered who he was with and what he was doing, and I would scour the house looking for clues. I searched his clothing, his wallet, his drawers, his boxes, his phone . . . I had become a slave to this nagging doubt that he would cheat again.

Eventually, he said he couldn't take it anymore, that he was working so hard to be good, and I just couldn't drop it. So we split. I went back home to my parents' home, humbled and brokenhearted. I knew I wouldn't be able to stay there long, so I saved up money and leased my own apartment.

We were broken up for two years, and during that time I started enjoying my freedom, but I was terrified to sleep alone. I was afraid of the dark, afraid of my neighbors, afraid that someone would break in . . . I was afraid *all the time*. My newfound singleness didn't last long. I quickly started dating another man, except this time I knew I didn't want anything serious—I just didn't want to be alone at night.

It didn't take long before Gary showed up again. Before long, he knew where I lived and spent the night with me on more than one occasion. He would show up drunk around three or four in the morning and expect to be let in. I would sometimes give in until we would have another explosive fight. A few days would go by, and then the cycle would begin again.

We were coming up on two years of this chaos and heartache when I decided to put my foot down and gave him an ultimatum. I told him that if we reached two years of being broken up and in the current state, I was going to shut him out of my life completely. I didn't want to be in limbo anymore. I threatened to move, change my number, and make sure he never saw me again. I told him we either got back together or moved on with our lives. That was the weekend he said goodbye.

I was shocked. I expected him to fight for me. I wanted him to love me enough to change for me and settle down with me. I never expected him to bring over the last of my belongings from his house and say farewell. That crushed me. I had grown accustomed to having him in my life. As messy, painful, and uncertain as our relationship was, I couldn't see myself without him forever. That Christmas was the saddest Christmas of my life. I didn't want to get out of bed. I couldn't even enjoy a night out with my girlfriends without ending up a teary, sloppy mess at the end of the night. It was quite the drama. That went on for about three months.

I finally started feeling better. I was motivated and excited about having true independence and freedom from our toxic relationship.

Well—it turned out to be just another one of our breaks. One afternoon, it happened: He started to call again. I couldn't believe it. I wanted my man back so severely, but when he reappeared, I was terrified to fall back into the same cycle we had been in for *four years*. He left several messages, sober for a change. He had been at a company conference in Catalina Island, and he missed me. In some of those messages, he described the beautiful scenery and told me, "The only thing missing to make this perfect is you, here with me." I melted. He was saying all the things I wanted him to tell me months earlier. He had a way with words when he was sober. He could quite literally convince me of *anything*.

I was once again at a crossroads: I could allow him back into my life, but it would mean taking a risk that we would fall back into our usual cycle. I was more than a little uncertain, but before long, I could no longer resist the urge to call him back and let him see me. We met for lunch one Friday afternoon. It was a casual lunch, and he asked if he could come over later that day. I agreed.

That evening, he showed up looking enticing with a new fade, a little mustache I had never seen before, and dressed to impress. He came for the evening and stayed the whole weekend. In the days that followed, he told me about how he was once again looking for a roommate. This time it was him who wanted me to move in. He didn't want to lose me and was ready to change. He promised me the world. He would be faithful and loyally devoted only to me.

He promised to be the man his parents raised him to be and the man I deserved. He was saying all the things I wanted to hear. He was painting the picture I had always envisioned in my mind for my life, one that included marriage to a man and beautiful children we would have together. He came back into my life just as I was considering dating women exclusively. As you know, I made my choice. I didn't fully believe all of his promises right away, but I was willing to take another chance with him.

We've been together ever since. But our story didn't move into Happily Ever After . . . not yet. He would have to earn my trust back in due time.

We had to go through a process of confronting and confessing our past to one another. He had questions and was disappointed that there had been other men in my life during our time apart. I blamed him for driving me into those relationships. At the time, I felt I was getting back at him for hurting me. In reality, I was only hurting myself as I gave myself away to men who didn't deserve me and only cared about themselves. I still had fears and a lot of anger due to all the lies and cheating. We knew we would have to air out all of our concerns and grieve before we could move forward in a healthy way. One morning, we agreed to have the conversation of all conversations. We would each have an opportunity to ask everything that was nagging at us, and the other would answer fully honest while we laid down our right to be angry for any new information that should come out. We also agreed to never bring up the past again. We agreed, and we had this heart-to-heart. That evening, we told each other everything we wanted or felt we needed to know about things that happened from the time we had met up until that moment. I got answers for even the most painful of questions. We made a conscious choice to be fully honest and to move forward together, choosing to forgive each other. We cried together and agreed to wipe the slate clean and move forward, fully loyal to one another and to the future we wanted to create together.

One day we took a shower together, and he proposed. It was spontaneous and vulnerable, and there was no ring. "Please be my wife?"

"What?"

"I don't have a ring, so don't tell anyone we're engaged. I'm working on that. But please agree you'll marry me. I promise to take care of you and be the man you deserve."

As you know, I said yes.

That was it. He never went back to his house except to pick up his clothes, and we began our life together.

Three months later, right at the beginning of spring, he took me out for a nice dinner at a steakhouse and a drive to the beach. He pulled over on Pacific Coast Highway, got down on one knee, and proposed with a diamond ring on a bluff overlooking the dark blue sea just beyond Malibu Beach.

And again, I said yes.

Our engagement season was beautiful. I was still sorting through my doubts and feelings and knew I needed to take some precautions, so I refused to leave my apartment. He would have to move out of the home we had been renting together and move into the apartment I had leased during our break-up. I felt I held more power and control if we were in my own domain. If we were going to try to work things out, there was no way I was going to allow him to put me out of our home again if things didn't work out. He had to move in with me. I also made sure we had a long engagement. I needed to test the waters and make sure the change he promised was for real. During our break, I had gone back to school and was nearly halfway through my bachelor's degree, so I asked him to wait until I graduated for us to get married. I told him I was afraid I'd get distracted and drop out again, and I didn't want to do that. He agreed, and we made it a two-and-a-half-year-long engagement. We were married one month after I graduated.

Life was exciting and fun. He made me laugh. He took me places I had never been. He spoiled me with expensive purses, shoes, and jewelry. Every weekend was a new adventure. We'd go out for lunch, talk over drinks until dinner, relocate to another place for the evening, and end up dancing somewhere elated and tipsy.

We were living in a bliss I wasn't familiar with. I still feared things could go back to how they were in the beginning—and they almost did.

We had agreed to start over and, going forward, our relationship was a process of maturing into the people we wanted to be and into the life we wanted to have: one that was peaceful, honest, and true. One that would withstand all storms and only grow stronger as a result of whatever struggle we overcame. That's what we have. Gary and I are now the happiest couple I know. Besides his parents, I had never known any one couple to respect and love each other honestly, humbly, and unconditionally.

Looking back, I see that God never left me, even when I said I was leaving Him. I rebelled and disobeyed all of God's laws, and life was not kind to me in return. I still have scars today that I carry as a result of the sinful choices of that very dark season of my life, but God has made all things new and is continuously pruning and strengthening my marriage.

When we choose to join ourselves physically with another, we open ourselves up to be influenced by their demons. Gary's alcoholism, promiscuity, and overall lack of self-control, in that season, led me to make bad choices of my own. Eventually, God redeemed our relationship, but it came with many mistakes and a whole lot of heart-ache in between. I now understand the importance of purity before marriage and why the church I attended during my college years was adamant about teaching and preserving purity in dating relationships. The Bible warns us against joining ourselves physically with others. By that sexual act, we become one flesh (1 Corinthians 6:16). These instructions are yet another principle meant to protect us from ourselves and this dark world.

INTIMATE WOUNDS

I swore I would never end up with an alcoholic and unfaithful husband, or in an abusive relationship. In the midst of all that beauty, however, alcohol was still an issue between us. I did not know I had the potential to become abusive myself, but it turned out the person I needed to protect my family from was me.

Many nights, after drinking heavily, we ended in explosive fights in which I insulted Gary and broke things he cared about. I was destructive, out of control, and full of rage in moments of frustration. When he overdid it, I was triggered back to my fear, and on more than one occasion, I said to him, "What? Are you going to hit me now?" The very thing I feared most was the thing I was expecting and even encouraging in our lives.

Time and again, he told me he would never touch me. Years went by before I believed him. I was critical, condescending, and always on guard. He often asked me, "Why are you so angry? I'm on your team."

I also made comments like, "Why don't you just leave?" I meant it too.

He would ask me, "When are you going to get it through your head? I'm on your team. I love you, and I'm never going to leave you."

I tested and tested and waited for the day he would finally hit me. I didn't know how to speak with him without being defensive and angry. He triggered my fears. His mere presence and tone of voice made me feel afraid. I didn't recognize it for years, and when I finally pieced it together, I was afraid to tell him. How would I be able to enjoy our life together if his mere masculinity sent me into defense and sometimes offensive behaviors for the sole purpose of protecting my heart from further wounding?

Fight-or-flight responses started to dominate our marriage and life. I didn't enjoy being around him, but I desperately wanted to be with him. He loved me, and he was kind and patient. Why couldn't I let my guard down and trust him? He was so good to me.

He repeated: "I'm not leaving; not today; not *ever.*" Despite the turbulence in our relationship, we had made a promise to God, and he was intent on keeping it. I didn't want to behave the way I did, but I didn't know how to resolve conflict or manage my fears or emotions.

We had things to work through, and we did. Early on in our marriage, we both knew we had things we needed to change about ourselves. He needed to stop drinking, and I needed to control my anger. We admitted it to ourselves and each other. With that honesty, we were able to understand and support each other better. Our marriage would not have lasted if we had not been honest and willing to put in the effort and make necessary changes even though those changes were hard to make.

He promised me he would stop drinking when we had kids. True to his word, he stopped shortly after I became pregnant with our first daughter. Sober, both of us had a better handle on our feelings and reactions and grew to rarely have reasons to fight. Over time, he proved himself to be trustworthy and, within that safety, I was able to tame my fears.

Thinking back on those early years—before we were married and had our girls—I know my childhood trauma was the reason I was terrified to end up with an alcoholic and abusive husband. I expected it because it was all I had seen growing up. I didn't know what a healthy marriage looked like that didn't involve some form of dysfunction. My mother's marriages had been dominated by alcoholism, violence, constant fighting, or cheating. I feared I was destined to continue the pattern. The cycle could have easily repeated.

With time, I began to see a destructive pattern in my behavior. Although I wouldn't admit it to myself or anyone else at the time, I could see I was sabotaging my marriage. I just didn't know how to change.

Healing childhood trauma is a process. I am telling you all of this because there may be areas of your own life in which you feel out of control. Maybe you are also triggered within your relationship and respond in ways you know are destructive, but you can't pinpoint the source or identify how to change them. You cannot fix what you don't know is broken. Awareness is a powerful tool. It is the first step toward change. I hope that reading my story so far helps you expose areas of your life where you may need healing. Once you are aware, you can begin to make changes. We will walk through how I was able to heal this area of my heart and marriage a little later in the book.

So far, you've read how my childhood abuse scarred me and set me up to operate out of fear, anger, and a lack of trust. In fact, those feelings and attitudes colored all of my close relationships. This is the reason I struggled to maintain long-term friendships. I always wanted a strong and loyal group of friends. Throughout the years, I went above and beyond to seek them out and nurture them. I gave all I could to create the kind of friendships I had always wanted, though my inability to trust made this nearly impossible. I sought to create something I didn't know how to do genuinely: be in safe and trusting relationships. My lack of experience with healthy relationships made it such that my friendships always ended as soon as someone disappointed or hurt me, or took me for granted. I would realize I was making most or all of the effort in the friendship and would eventually shut them out before they had an opportunity to hurt me further. It was isolating.

—————————— Healing Exercise 1.2 ——————————

1. It is time to do some self-reflection. We cannot repair what we don't recognize is broken. We also cannot change others, but we can certainly make a conscious choice and effort to change how we respond to outside circumstances and how we respond to stresses within our relationships.

Do you see an area of your life that may have been affected by some of the experiences you noted in Exercise 1.1?
Journal your thoughts.

CHAPTER 7

Motherhood and Memories

All along God was setting me up for the win. Ultimately, it was my love for my husband and my children that led me to see the harm my trauma was still causing me. My family, who by no fault of their own, became mine and deserved better. I wanted to protect them and give them the best wife and mother possible, but I needed to be healthy in order to offer that. God places us in families for a reason. We are meant to represent God. It's through my family that I experienced unconditional love for the first time, and it is through them that I learned to love unconditionally.

My first pregnancy was magical. I felt connected to my husband of one year in a way that can only be described as the "honeymoon stage." It truly was. We always knew we wanted to have children but had planned on traveling and enjoying the early years of our marriage, getting to know each other on a deeper level. That was the plan anyway.

In reality, my maternal clock started ticking the moment we said, "I do." Only a few months into our marriage, I decided I was ready to become a mother, so I began my mission to detox and prepare my body to bring forth life. The conditions were ideal. I was twenty-nine years old, married to the man of my prayers, and as healthy as they come. I was in the best shape of my life at the time, running four-and-a-half miles at least three times per week, and I was working with a personal trainer I had hired before the wedding to get me ready for my big day. I gave up alcohol and smoking weed, and had switched to an organic diet.

That February, as we celebrated love as a married couple for the first time, we conceived our firstborn daughter. My pregnancy was easy. I was a little queasy and required a slice of chocolate cake almost daily, but other than that, my only concern was slowing down my exercise routine, per the doctor's orders.

The day labor began, my husband and I had decided to go on our final date night before the baby arrived. We went to dinner at a local favorite of mine and to a movie. I sat there the entire time noticing the tightening of my belly and recognizing that these minor contractions felt different from those I had experienced throughout my pregnancy. The tightening turned into a small ache that persisted throughout the movie and only intensified ever so slightly.

As the evening progressed, I knew the time had come. That night, I stayed up timing and tracking contractions, and the next day they went at much the same pace. It was clear we were in labor. I had taken the classes and read all about the labor process, so I knew what was happening. I had heard stories of women being in the hospital laboring for forty-eight hours, sometimes more, and I was not going to do that. My "birth plan" was specific: I was to arrive at the hospital when my contractions were ten minutes apart (as suggested by my doctor) or when the pain was unbearable (that was my preference). I was certain I wanted to experience the early stages of labor in the comfort of my home. We lived only five minutes away from the hospital where I was to deliver, so my doctor did not have any concerns with that plan.

Truth be told, I barely made it. Because I have a high tolerance for pain, and being a first-time mother, I misjudged how far along I was in the process.

My husband had gone out to buy us some Pupusas. A pregnant lady ready to give birth needs nourishment! When he arrived, the smell of the melty, greasy goodness overpowered the house, and I couldn't take it. Seeing that I was getting ready to vomit, he rushed to my rescue, ready to catch it with both hands like a true gentleman. He managed to bathe me in it instead. *Uh oh—I'm pretty sure I read somewhere that vomit means crowning,* I thought to myself. *Awesome, but first I needed a shower!*

At that point, I was in intense pain—the kind of pain that stops you in your tracks. The contractions became really severe in the shower. The car ride was unbearable. I was literally writhing in pain. When we attempted to check into Labor & Delivery, I couldn't even speak. I was rolled into our room and asked questions in bed.

Another important part of my birth plan was that I would not be taking any pain medication. I wanted to fully experience all the pain and glory of childbirth, just as my mother and her mother had done. In my mind, we were created to give life, and labor pain was an important part of that journey for me.

One of the first things I was asked was if I wanted an epidural, to which I responded, "Well, that depends: How much more of this do I have to go?" I was ready to reconsider and give up on my all-natural plan if I was going to remain in that degree of agony!

"Well," the nurse said, "let's check." I had arrived in the hospital fully dilated. "Oh honey, you're done," she said. "This baby is coming any minute. I'm surprised you didn't have her in the car!"

"What?!" I was shocked.

"Let me know when you're ready to push," she continued.

"How do I know if I am ready to push?" I asked.

"Oh, you'll know."

As the nurse looked away to continue checking me in, I knew it was time to push! I had been in the hospital less than forty minutes when Aaliyah was born. It was the happiest day of my life. She's perfect! It's true what they say: The minute you hold them, you forget all about how they had literally split you in two right down the middle just seconds before.

I knew I wanted my daughters to grow up together and to be close in age so that they would have a best friend for life. They would never have to be alone—they would have each other. Aaliyah was a little over one year old when I told my husband I wanted to have another. I was still nursing, not sleeping, and exhausted from the rush-hour commute to my office in downtown Los Angeles. We had just purchased the home we planned to raise them in, so this seemed like an ideal time.

It didn't take long. We were blessed with both our children. Once we said we wanted a baby, God immediately granted our desire. It took only two or three months from conversation to conception with both of our children. Being pregnant with a toddler was rough. There was no way I could nap whenever I felt like it; there was a little one at my breast around the clock still, and she required a ton of attention.

Nothing could have prepared us to get the news that something was not right in my womb.

I was at work one afternoon when I got a phone call from my doctor's office. Over the phone they told me something was abnormal with my umbilical cord and that the last ultrasound had also found a spot on my daughter's heart.

The news floored me. I scrambled, making my way over to my car where I could openly cry. I called my husband and told him. I called my boss and told her something had come up, and I needed to leave. I don't know how I made it home that day. I was in despair.

Further analysis and conversations with my doctor revealed that my umbilical cord had not formed properly. Most babies have one vein to bring in nutrients from the placenta and two arteries to take waste from the baby back to the placenta. In my case, I had the vein and one artery instead of two. That meant that the umbilical cord would be strained throughout the pregnancy with one artery doing the work of two.

The pregnancy was high risk and stressful. We were told the baby may not grow to the weight it should. There was also a possibility the baby would not thrive in the third trimester and that I may not make it to full term.

We were also told that these two concerns were considered markers for children with genetic disabilities and that it was possible the baby could be born with down syndrome. We were presented with the option to have a series of further tests, which included an amniocentesis, a test which uses a long hollow needle to extract amniotic fluid from the uterus to test for abnormalities in the baby. This test is risky, and we knew the risk could be catastrophic; in some cases, the amniotic sack ruptures, at which point I could have lost the baby. The whole pregnancy, we were threatened with the risk of a preterm delivery and with the risk of a small baby that may or may not make it to term. I also struggled with my asthma and couldn't breathe most of the pregnancy. At the same time, I was commuting two hours in each direction to and from my office downtown. It was all very stressful.

We had gone from bliss to high stress in a matter of just a couple years. We feared for our daughter's life in the womb, and we had a difficult choice to make at that point: test the baby so that we could know what to expect and how to prepare ourselves for a baby with special needs if necessary, or go through the pregnancy hoping for the best. If the baby made it to full term, it was possible we would discover at birth that our baby would have special needs. This was yet another fork in the road where I knew one choice could alter our future.

Fortunately, we had a doctor ask us the most important question: "If your baby is found to have down syndrome or some other genetic disability, will you have an abortion?" That question quickly settled it for us. We did not move forward with any further analysis for genetic issues and prayed God would deliver us a healthy baby girl.

I don't want you to feel judged if you have made a choice contrary to the one we made. God loves you, and there is nothing he cannot heal you from, even this.

We were blessed to have a perfectly healthy baby girl. She didn't just make it to term, she went past her due date one week. The doctors basically wanted to force her out, but I didn't allow it. I told them, "She'll be born when she's good and ready." Alyssa was perfect, and she came to complete our family. Our little miracle is amazing in every way. Both of my children are miracles.

NEW CHALLENGES

Right around the time our little Alyssa was born, my oldest baby girl appeared to be delayed in achieving some of her milestones, and someone suggested we should have her evaluated for a developmental disability.

"What?" I was offended and defensive. How dare they tell me something was wrong with my daughter.

She was two and wasn't yet speaking, and she showed no signs of even being close to ready for potty training. We had tried that and quickly given up.

That season was the hardest season of my life; all of the pain and struggles I had suffered at the hands of others, and those which I brought on myself, did not compare to the pain of having something happen to my children.

We reluctantly moved into a series of intense evaluations and therapies for our little girl to help her develop her speech and language abilities and to track all her milestones to confirm or refute the idea that she may have some genetic disorder.

We went from stressing, waiting, and hoping for the best for our baby to stressing, waiting, and hoping for our oldest baby girl. We were tracking what they call autistic-like behaviors, some of which persist today. Ultimately, we found out that our daughter does have a mild learning disability. She is social, sweet, creative, compassionate, and oh-so-loving, but she struggles in academics, recognizing the spacial distance between objects, and some physical activities. Learning and development has been hard, but she continues to surprise us. Nonetheless, she is perfect, albeit quirky, and we are so blessed that God entrusted both of these babies to us.

Those early years parenting our children in the midst of so much uncertainty and stress were hard. We weren't getting enough sleep and had not been out alone as individuals, or as a couple, since our children were born. I entered a difficult season of dissatisfaction, and my heart became bitter. Where we should have been leaning into each other as a couple, it felt as though a wall had been raised between us. We began to fight, blame, and avoid one another.

So many times, we knew we needed help, but something kept us paralyzed: fear, guilt, disappointment . . . so many things kept us stuck in a place of dissatisfaction. For me, that dissatisfaction led to bitterness and self-centeredness. We became consumed with "I," "me," and "my" needs, wants, and desires and how they were not being met by the other. This bitterness pitted us against each other when what we needed was to remember that we were a team.

Dissatisfaction led me to a very dangerous place, and I started to realize the thin ice I was treading on. I was exhausted from the stresses and challenges of motherhood and marriage, and I was also unfulfilled in my career. It's in these seasons of overwhelm and dissatisfaction that we need to be most careful because it's in these seasons that our heart and our life are at greatest risk.

Be careful of what you allow in your thoughts. Dissatisfaction in marriage can fester and grow to dangerous levels. Throughout my life, I watched my mother's unhealed trauma lead her to bitterness that led her to physically beat me throughout my youth and a toxic family environment that I can almost guarantee had traumatic effects on my siblings as well. She also cheated multiple times. I seriously considered the emotional ramifications of including this part of our story in this book because I love and respect my mother and would never want to hurt her. I decided to include it after requesting her permission because I feel it is important to illustrate the devastating ripple effects of unresolved trauma and the grave danger of allowing dissatisfaction to grow in our marriages. As you read, my mother escaped a physically and emotionally abusive marriage to my father by leaving him for a neighbor. Twenty-three years later, she left my stepfather for a man she worked with. While the first affair saved us from the life of violence that had already scarred us severely, the second affair completely shattered our family. After years of lying, hiding and being discovered by her children, my mother finally left with her boyfriend, leaving only a note behind. This didn't surprise us but it was devastating nonetheless. I never expected the experience to shake me the way it did. After all, I was an adult woman, married with children of my own but it did. Eight years later, we are still trying to pick up the pieces and adjust to split Christmases, birthdays, and the resentment and pain that each of our parents are still dealing with. It has taken an emotional toll on all of us, young to old.

Infidelity is the source of ruin of many marriages. I am determined not to repeat with my own family what I witnessed in my childhood. We all have great potential for harm, and I have chosen to fight for my marriage. Adultery has devastating consequences, and it will destroy your life (Proverbs 6:26; Jeremiah 7:9-10). It is the atomic bomb that sends many marriages to ruin and children into emotional turmoil, causing wounds that harm them well into their adult lives. Protect your family, but if you have made this mistake, know that God will forgive you still (John 8:1-11), so take heart—this, too, can be healed.

SHAME SURFACES

When I had arrived at a calm marriage, I thought I had overcome my trauma. The truth is, I was only halfway through the tunnel. Giving birth to daughters was like throwing salt on an open wound. Once again, I arrived at a season that was new and difficult. Motherhood magnified my fears and anxieties in unexpected ways.

The day my first daughter was born, I changed her diaper for the first time and realized the abuse I had suffered had wounded me profoundly. Seeing her naked body reminded me of how vulnerable she was. I was terrified of seeing and touching her. I didn't bathe her for a whole month when she was first born. When I finally bathed her, I poured water over her from a distance with a cup. This tormented me for years.

My memories were triggered; I remembered what had happened to me and felt terrified that it could happen to them. Then, I felt ashamed and disgusted with myself for having these thoughts and for my inability to control my memories. Too ashamed and terrified to form the idea into words even in my mind, I kept fighting the thoughts and was unable to stop them. What began to materialize over time was a terrible fear that I could be a threat to my own children. The thought made me want to vomit. I knew I would never harm my children; I shaped my whole life around protecting them. So why did I have this nagging feeling that they weren't safe—not even with me? What did that mean? How could I stop the thoughts? Was I destined to struggle with this awful NEW secret?

I struggled with this for years with both of my daughters. I felt disgusted with myself for having the thoughts. *What is this?* I wondered. *Is it that their bodies trigger my memories, and the feelings in my body associated with the abuse I experienced? Did I damage my brain so badly experimenting with women that I cannot even look at my own daughters? Is it a tendency? Is it an urge? What is it?* I realized that this thing, whatever it was, was tormenting, haunting, and ultimately tainting my relationship with my children.

Although I knew I could never do anything to harm my children, I fought these thoughts unsuccessfully for nearly a decade. It was when I realized that I was powerless to stop the memories and thoughts that I turned to God. I finally told a dear friend in confidence that I was struggling with cleaning and caring for my daughters. She told me she was struggling with the same issue with her son. She also told me about the sexual abuse she had experienced as a child. Once I realized that another young mom was struggling similarly in the mothering of her children, I came to understand that this struggle was an effect of the sexual abuse that we experienced when we were young. I knew then and there that it was not specific only to me. This realization released us from the shame we felt over those intrusions with our children. Sharing those struggles with each other helped us to get free. I realized later that it was a consequence not only of the sins committed against me but of the sins I committed as a result as well.

In an attempt to try to understand what had happened in my youth, and how I was affected at the time, I ordered my school transcripts. The day they arrived from the Los Angeles Unified School District (LAUSD), I also told my husband about the thoughts I was having around my girls, and I started to cry. *"It's not fair that I have these thoughts! It's not fair that I can't look at my girls and that I feel ashamed to bathe them! It's not right! Am I going to live with the residue of childhood sexual abuse my whole life? Maybe! I guess this was just the life I was given. Maybe This will be a burden my entire life. Maybe I will struggle with this my whole life. God promised He would cleanse us, heal us, and set us free.*

He promised he would renew our minds. That's what I need . . . that's what I need so badly!"

When I said it out loud, that's when it happened. I realized that this thing had a power over me that I could not stop, that it elicited feelings of shame, and that I felt prone to harm my children. And although I knew I would never hurt my children, I simply couldn't stop those thoughts from interrupting my time alone with them. The realization that I could not stop these thoughts from interfering in my life and with my children, and my crying out to God and proclaiming His promises over my life, was where I finally found freedom.

CHAPTER 8

Hebrews 10

My season of healing began with me telling people I trusted about what happened to me. After sharing my experience with that trusted friend, and finding that we struggled with similar scars of abuse in our parenting, I vulnerably expressed to my husband the ongoing struggle I was having in my mind over the memories and the residual fear that was influencing my thoughts, relationships, and marriage. Speaking out loud about those experiences brought the feelings I had buried long ago into the light. It was painful and overwhelming, but I had my husband as a committed listener. He received what I was revealing and held me through that difficult moment. But it was crying out to God in the midst of my pain and proclaiming His biblical promises over my life that began the breakthrough season of my life. That night changed everything. That was the moment that led to the radical transformation I experienced. Crying out to God started a domino effect and set the wheels in motion for my spiritual and emotional healing to occur.

After everyone fell asleep that night, I walked into the living room with the intention of watching television. I desperately wanted to clear my mind and reflect on something different before going to sleep. God had other plans. As I went to sit down on our sofa, I sensed the voice of God in an obvious way. Something inside me said:

"Don't turn on the TV. Open your Bible."

I hesitated. I was exhausted from the emotional day I had had. I just wanted to relax for a moment and think of nothing.

Again, I heard Him say:

"Don't miss this opportunity; your Father has something to say."

I decided to obey but told Him that wherever the application landed when I opened it, that was what I was going to read. I opened the Bible application on my phone and found it in Hebrews 10.

Hebrews 10 was the key that unlocked my healing, *ONCE FOR ALL TIME.*

I began to read it and knew immediately that God had sent me there for a reason. In it, the scripture speaks of Jesus as the perfect sacrifice for sin. His body was the ultimate offering and the only sacrifice that can remove our feelings of guilt. He cleansed our sin once for all time through His death on the cross.

For God's will was for us to be made holy by the sacrifice
of the body of Jesus Christ, once for all time.
– Hebrews 10:10 (NLT)

I read it and was shocked. He was speaking to me directly and clearly, giving me exactly what I needed to know. "Once for all time" were the words that stood out to me the most. "Once for all time." I read it over and over again.

Wait – that means . . . He has already taken this from me.

I needed to arrive at the point where I understood and embraced that truth. I thanked Him for His loving sacrifice and forgiveness.

This is the number one thing I want you to remember from this whole book—He has already taken this from you. All of it. *Once for all time.*

You need to know that you are not a danger to your children if you are struggling with the memories. Those memories are a part of your experience, and perhaps they will always be with you, but your mind can be renewed. God already took this from you, and now He wants to heal you from it. If this is something you struggle with too, take solace in this scripture. He already took this from you. That's why He died that painful death so that you wouldn't have to carry this burden. He wants you to accept that, let it soak in, embrace it, and choose to walk in that truth. For more on how to heal toxic memories, I recommend *Switch on Your Brain* by Dr. Caroline Leaf.[4]

GOD THE FATHER WILL HEAL EVEN OUR FATHER WOUNDS

Exactly three days later, it was Easter Sunday, and we were at church with my in-laws. After the service, we went to their home to spend the afternoon. I got into a deep conversation with my father-in-law. I opened up about my abuse and told him I wanted to be restored by God.

He asked me, "Karla, tell me: What happens when you repair a car?"

"It breaks again," I answered.

"Exactly," he responded. "God works differently. *God doesn't only want to restore you; HE HAS MADE YOU NEW. Open your Bible to Hebrews 10.*"

WHAT?! There was God again, pointing to Jesus and the forgiveness He purchased for us on the cross. At that moment, I knew God was speaking to me through my father-in-law because three nights earlier, He had also instructed me to open my Bible to the same scripture. I was perplexed. God was telling me once again: *You are a new creation. I have already taken this from you.*

---

[4] Leaf, Dr. Caroline. *Switch on Your Brain: The Key to Peak Happiness, Thinking, and Health.* Michigan: Baker Books, 2013.

BRINGING MY FATHER WOUNDS
TO OUR LOVING FATHER ─────────────────

I also told my father-in-law I felt like an orphan. I had never had a father who I could rely on for support and godly guidance. My mother leaned on me for guidance and support growing up. This is difficult for me to say, and it might be difficult to hear for those of you who truly have lost your parents. I might sound completely ungrateful, but the truth is, I didn't have the godly instruction I needed as a child. My parents were unable to provide the unconditional, selfless, wise instruction and love that children need to grow up strong and healthy.

If you can relate to this, or if you have lost your parents, I'm truly sorry for your loss. I'm sorry if this is difficult to talk about, but please bear with me. You need to know that, although you and I were orphans either in spirit or in reality, *God is your Father*. He wants to hold you, comfort you, guide you, and give you wisdom to transcend all time. He also wants to place you in His family.

And there are people around you who love you, and who you can turn to for comfort, godly guidance, and support.

That night after reading that scripture, my father-in-law asked if he could pray for me. After we prayed, he gave me the biggest hug he had ever given me. With tears running down his cheeks, he said, "I'm so sorry for what happened to you." He told me, "You are not alone. Don't ever feel as though you are. We are here for you. We love you. Please take good care of our granddaughters. We don't want anything bad to happen to them."

Something miraculous happened when my father-in-law told me, "You are a new creation." There was a point in our conversation when I felt like God himself was speaking through him. The Bible tells us that the Holy Spirit empowers us and that we should speak with confidence as though He himself is speaking through us (Matthew 10:20). I felt like I, too, was resurrected on that Resurrection Sunday. I am in no way comparing myself to Jesus—far from it—but I felt like I stepped into the next level of my healing, as though something heavy fell from me and I was walking as God's new and perfect creation. He gave me a new life, and I was ready to live as such.

God seeks us in surprising ways. If we allow Him, He meets us right where we are and gives us what we didn't even know we needed. God used my husband's father to fill such a void in my heart. I feel like my Father in Heaven gave me a father on earth! As Jesus did for Mary when He knew He was leaving her, He gave her a new family.

> *When Jesus saw his mother standing there beside the disciple*
> *He loved, He said to her, "Dear woman, here is your son."*
> *And He said to this disciple, "Here is your mother."*
> *— John 19:26-27*

When our earthly father hurts us, neglects, us, or abandons us, we gain a distorted image of family and are unable to see God's love for what it is. He wants not only to repair what was broken; He wants to make you whole and to place you in a spiritual family too.

That night in conversation with my husband's father, I realized that God had given me spiritual parents in my in-laws. They have been loving me consistently and unconditionally for years. They are who I lean on when I need anything. My husband travels a lot for work and is also in school. Somehow, whenever something breaks at home—a pipe for example—it always happens while he is away. When I find myself in need of help, I call my father-in-law. He drops whatever he is doing, runs to the store, and is at our house within the hour repairing whatever was broken. The fact that healing my father wounds came to me through my father-in-law is very symbolic and meaningful.

Regardless of our unique experiences, we can all agree that life is not easy. However, God places people in our lives to help us carry the load of our struggles. My lack of trust in people made it so that I relied only on myself to care for, provide, and nurture my family. Turning away from my children for even a moment was an extremely difficult thing. It's why my marriage also suffered early on; I didn't think I had people around me whom I could trust to help. Meanwhile, my in-laws were there, yearning for more time with their grandchildren and loving us from a distance. It wasn't until God started walking me toward healing that I recognized what my in-laws were offering was a truly unconditional love. It was then that I allowed myself to lean on them for support, guidance, and help.

My mother-in-law is now the first person we ask when it comes to watching our girls. She knew I struggled with trust even before I shared anything about my past. She once offered to watch our children so that Gary and I could go out for dinner alone, and slowly I began to trust her more and more. Gary and I were also reminded on those outings that we were once crazy about each other and really enjoyed each other's company. Hidden underneath the stress was a couple who missed each other and desired to connect deeply again.

———————————— Healing Exercise 1.3 ————————————

I encourage you to begin to think of relationships in a new way. God has placed certain people in your life to love and serve you well. Perhaps you have not been able to see it because of a fear and difficulty with trusting others. I completely understand. I was there once. It's okay to be cautious. You do not need to give anyone complete access into your life. Consider this: Are there areas of your life where you have been holding back in relationships as a means of self-protection?

Who are the people in your life who have been there for you in the past to love and support you in any way they could? Could they be the kind of people who could lighten your load if only you would allow them to be there for you? Journal your thoughts. We'll come back to this later.

CHAPTER 9

A Leap of Faith

He has made everything beautiful in its time.
– Ecclesiastes 3:11 (NIV)

My career was also impacted and limited by the wounds of my past. I once had an inappropriate relationship with a boss. He was someone I admired and trusted. He mentored me, and I cared about him deeply, but he also complimented me and attempted to seduce me. I didn't recognize this at the time, but he groomed me (just as I had been groomed when I was a child). He told me he was going to teach me everything he knew and help me get elected into a political office one day. I was young and naive, and when someone of such stature believed in me, I was mesmerized. The perception was that I had not earned my position rightfully. And, on some level, I know that was true. This man offered me a wonderful opportunity, albeit with the wrong intentions, and I accepted it. The rumor went around that I had had an affair with this man. I did not; however, the relationship was inappropriate in that I allowed the advances, enjoyed them, and benefitted from the relationship. I remained silent, and the employment opportunity changed my life financially. The choice I made had tremendous consequences in my professional life.

There were times I met people who addressed me with so much disdain right away. I would introduce myself, and they would say,

"Oh—I know who you are." I felt so much shame; my reputation was tarnished. This experience remained a dark cloud that followed me for years. I was only freed from it once I left that organization.

I didn't know it then, but I can see it now: When a little girl learns early that affection equals sexual touching, it becomes tough to say NO. NO isn't even part of the conversation. I had lost my power and didn't realize it.

Years later, I once again found myself in a position in which I was being noticed and complimented by someone in a managerial position. This man was a mid-level manager with a reputation for being a flirt. It was no secret that he often lingered, hovering over the cubicle desks of attractive young women. It made us all very uncomfortable, and we often discussed it amongst ourselves during our lunch breaks.

I had experienced it as well, but wasn't too concerned by it until he became my direct supervisor. As a result of an organizational shift, I was transferred to a field office closer to home. The proximity of this new location to my house was ideal. However, there were days when he and I were the only ones working in our small office, and my discomfort grew. I did not invite or enjoy the compliments I was getting, and I made it known. The environment became tense.

One day, while no one else was there, he openly commented on my physical appearance, and I decided I was not going to allow it. I had learned from my earlier experience years before. This time, I did not remain silent. I made the bold choice to tell my then-supervisor. She made the statement that he was too smart to do such a thing, and I felt forced to go above her, directly to our human resources department. My representative filed a written report and told me it would be investigated.

I was then asked what I hoped for by bringing it to their attention. I was shocked that I was asked such a question. I was unprepared for it. I expected it was they who would know and pursue the appropriate course of action. I requested a transfer to another division and building. It was granted, and things continued as usual for him. I knew going forward that saying something had labeled me as a problem employee. The organization was known to transfer problems to other divisions.

He remained a manager, and his reputation and demeanor remain to this day.

Women begin experiencing abuse at a very young age and throughout our lives—at least until we find our voice and courage, and set up unshakeable boundaries. Speaking up about the subtle and abusive behavior was uncomfortable, but it raised up a shield of protection for me. When I spoke up about the compliments I was receiving from my manager, I established myself as someone who was not to be toyed with. Using my voice in this way became a strong deterrent of abuse going forward. Similarly, with my voice, I also put a stop to the abuse I was experiencing at the hands of my uncle so long ago. This is what I learned from that experience: Men will hesitate to initiate any form of misconduct toward women if they think they will be exposed.

It was a tough lesson that took a long time for me to arrive at, but that knowledge was worth the discomfort of those early workplace experiences. I now know how powerful my voice is.

Numerous studies suggest that sexual victimization in adolescence significantly increases the likelihood of sexual victimization in adulthood.[5] Further, when a child is given male attention from a young age to gain access to and exploit her body, she adopts an incorrect association between affection and sexuality. Those of us with a history of childhood sexual abuse learned incorrectly that our worth is tied to our bodies and what we have to offer men physically. The lies we adopt from our abuse and the persistence of sexual harassment in the workplace go hand in hand. This is a strong statement to be sure, but there is evidence all around us that our culture has reduced women to objects for male entertainment. Just look at the sexually explicit nature of much of the content in music, advertising, and television. The inappropriate association we've made between affection and sexualized relationships (as a result of our childhood abuse), coupled with our culture's obsession with women as sexual objects, inadvertently places women in a position of powerlessness in the workplace. We may know that advances by men

---

[5] "Sexual Revictimization." NSVRC. https://www.nsvrc.org/sites/default/files/2012-06/publications_NSVRC_ResearchBrief_Sexual-Revictimization.pdf.

in positions of authority are inappropriate and morally wrong, but may lack the self-confidence to say NO; and, as a result, we may allow men to go further than we are comfortable.

Statistics tell us that women who have experienced abuse are prone to re-experience abuse again later. Additionally, research supports the idea that some female childhood sexual abuse victims adopt harmful beliefs about sexuality leading them to believe that coercion and trauma are normal characteristics of sexual relations. This leads them to have a higher tolerance for intimidating sexual advances, which leaves them vulnerable to revictimization. In a recent survey of 64,000 employees by LeanIn.org and McKinsey & Co., more than one in three of the women surveyed indicated they had been harassed in their careers.[6]

This has been my experience. Most women can relate to at least some of the examples above. Non-violent forms of abuse can feel subtle. There is a part of us that tells us it is wrong, but we don't feel we have the power to stop them.

Also, we may not recognize it at first, but these experiences plant shame deep within us, and that shame can influence us later, causing us to make bad choices. Again, the allowances we make are rooted in the lies we adopted about ourselves as a result of the abuse we experienced.

This does not in any way diminish the importance of us also being responsible for the choices we have made of our own free will. More on that later.

The spotlight has been placed on this pervasive issue affecting every rank of our workplace culture. As a society, some are struggling to understand, while others seek to improve the problem systemically.

Meanwhile, survivors (some who may not have been ready to address their personal pain) are faced with the challenge of being reminded almost daily of their own traumatic experiences with very little dialogue or direction given about the road to healing.

---

[6] Furhmans, Vanessa. "What #MeToo Has to Do with the Workplace Gender Gap." *The Wall Street Times.* 23 October 2018. https://www.wsj.com/articles/what-metoo-has-to-do-with-the-workplace-gender-gap-1540267680

If this is your story, you may recognize now that the sexual abuse you experienced when you were a child affected you in more ways than you knew. You should also acknowledge that you were powerless as a child, and that powerlessness shaped how you responded to circumstances that presented themselves later in life.

As a child, you were powerless to discern, stop, or consent to the sexual advances of the men who abused you. The gifts, attention, and affection you received may have been welcomed; you were a child. You did not know the love you were receiving was a conditional type of love meant to condition you to remain silent. Similar dynamics are at play in our adult lives. As with the example I shared above from early in my career. Consider the obvious power differential. We don't always question or speak out against this dynamic; we learned this behavior and powerlessness early on.

You should also know that the shame you have carried all these years for what you experienced when you were too young to provide consent—be it in your primary school or teenaged years—is not yours to carry. Place the responsibility for it where it rightfully belongs—in the hands of the person(s) who abused you.

If you are feeling guilty for choices you made later of your own free will: Guilt is a gift from God that helps us recognize that we've made a mistake. It is given to us for the purpose of bringing us back into right standing with Him. Lean into that feeling and allow it to serve its rightful purpose. He wants to cleanse you, forgive you, and free you of your guilty conscience.

As an adult, you can take your power back by releasing responsibility for the evil choices of others, while taking responsibility for the guilt you feel for the decisions you made as a result. Be honest with yourself, confess it to God, ask Him for forgiveness, and choose to be different going forward. Stand firmly in your true identity. You were wonderfully made in the image of God. You are a princess in the eyes of your Creator, and you should be treated as such. Take back your power: Protect your body and heart by placing firm boundaries and standing in your worth.

Again, some of the allowances we make in our adult lives are rooted in the lies we adopted about ourselves as a result of the abuse we experienced, but this does not in any way diminish the importance of us also being responsible for our own choices of our own free will. As such, we need to take responsibility for the *guilt* we feel for our sins, *confess* them to God, ask for *forgiveness*, and *choose* to be different going forward (*repent*). I'll say more about this later on in the book.

Despite these challenges, I worked hard and reached levels of success in my career. I met some wonderful mentors and friends and received amazing opportunities. I want to encourage you to make the most of leadership training opportunities in your workplace and others you can participate with on your own time. Early in my career, a friend encouraged me to apply to the Hispanas Organized for Political Equity (HOPE) Latina Leadership Institute (HLI). HOPE is a non-profit advocacy organization that promotes opportunities for the advancement of Latinas. The HLI provides Latina professionals from diverse industry sectors training in leadership and advocacy skills. Training is designed to equip them with tools to become effective leaders in their neighborhoods, professions, and throughout California. HOPE influences the lives of the women it serves by providing leadership skills and empowering them to be active and engaged in their communities. Through education and experiential learning, these women become stronger and more influential. HOPE's impacts are permanent, far-reaching, and transcend generations. By empowering a woman, HOPE is transforming entire families and future generations. This educational opportunity opened my eyes to a world of possibilities, and connected me with a network of hundreds of Latina leaders. I met many wonderful women as part of the HOPE network. I have seen these women grow and thrive in their careers, and over the years wonderful mentorship relationships have evolved.

Despite the opportunity and role models I gained as a result, I spent many years stagnant and dissatisfied. I was on my own journey and needed to grow into a genuine confidence within myself. It took years for me to find the courage I needed to reach for my dreams. Eventually the HOPE organization and the women continued to be supportive. I remained connected and attended their annual conference, which always gave me a boost of energy and excitement. The leadership training and mentorship from other successful women built me up over the years, but without a strong faith, I lacked the courage and direction to reach for the success I desired. Eventually it was through HOPE that I was introduced to my first coach, the woman who helped me pursue my purpose and the goal of writing this book. I will share more about how this unfolded soon.

After I discovered HOPE, I continued to advance my career. For nearly twenty years, I managed community programs that helped to improve the lives of women and families in Los Angeles. For several of those years, I secured increasing levels of responsibility within exciting projects and programs. Eventually, my career seemed to reach a ceiling, and I couldn't move past it. I had experience, education, and leadership skills, but something prevented me from boldly stepping into the leadership position I desired. I couldn't figure out what it was. I didn't know it then, but I see now that fear and a lack of self-confidence were preventing me from achieving the potential I knew I had inside. I knew I needed to make a change, but fear kept me unable to move forward.

The career I had nurtured throughout my adult life was all I knew. Still, I wasn't sure if I wanted to continue on that path anymore. The what-ifs and potential disasters we create in our minds can be utterly paralyzing. I was terrified of losing all I had built. What would I do if I left my work in government? Was it too late in my life to change direction and do something entirely different? Could my family continue to sustain the lifestyle we were accustomed to if I chose to start over? I asked myself these questions over and over without moving forward in any direction.

On the outside, I was confident, secure, and beautifully polished. I spent hours every day putting myself together and creating an outward appearance of strength. I had already accomplished far more than I had ever imagined and didn't know how to move to the next level because I couldn't see it. Lacking a vision of success, I could not pave the way for my future self. It wasn't that I wasn't motivated.

I was dissatisfied with my work and felt it didn't have the impact it should. I started to questions if I was walking in my purpose and didn't think so. For years, I had been fighting the tension to launch into something new and different. I was in the government box of my career and didn't think I could do anything else. I was giving all my energy at work, yet it wasn't appreciated or valued. I was arriving at home with nothing left to give my family but a cranky, over-worked dictator. I had to make a choice.

We tend to turn to God for help and comfort in our most desperate and fearful moments.

I began to pray. I asked God to show me the way and give me the courage to leap forward in a new direction. What I didn't know was that He was making the way for me all along. God knows our hearts and our deepest needs better than we do ourselves. He wants to give us our best life. It takes struggle and disappointment for us to see how much we need Him! I'm blessed to have a husband who believes in me and supports *all* of my dreams. Together, we decided it was time for me to take a break from work and figure out my next move. We made the bold decision to trust God fully for our financial provision, and I decided to quit my job.

When I took my "leap of faith," however, I was at the lowest point in my career. I was at the brink of being fired when I made the decision to move on. I had succeeded for a time, but the pace was excruciating. My organization valued high performance over people, and they were mean. I also felt invisible. And, when I began to speak up about the workload being excessive and the unfair treatment from my immediate supervisor, I was told, "If you can't handle it, there is the door." That meeting marked the beginning of then end. I was then placed under a microscope and it was clear that I was being targeted and squeezed out.

I could see that the relationship with this organization was not going to end well. I knew that I needed to leave or risk being fired. I made the decision to be the one to end it because I thought, at least this way I could leave with my dignity intact and on my own terms or timing.

It was the boldest decision of my life.

I gave them my two-week notice, and I knew I had made the right choice because of the weight that was immediately lifted from my being. However, I was unable to complete my final two weeks because they made my last day immediately after my exit interview. I was completely honest in my evaluation of management, and, shortly after, I received a call in which I was told, "Tomorrow will be your last day."

That felt like a punch in the stomach. They still had to have the last word.

The world may call that moment a failure, in reality, it was the best thing that could have happened. God had been trying to redirect me for years, but I was too afraid to listen. He needed to turn up the pressure to get me to move in the direction He wanted me to go. I am no longer afraid to fail. I needed to experience that moment so that I could arrive at this moment. I have experienced failure, and I am stronger than ever before.

What the enemy meant to discourage and belittle me, God used for good.

For the first time in my life, I jumped into the unknown with both feet and eyes closed, and trusted that God would catch and carry me. Little did I know, God was going to use this time to reveal and heal all of the brokenness inside of me. I was scared, but full of excitement for the opportunity to slow down, clear my mind, and evaluate whether or not my life was on the correct path. When I took the leap out of the workforce, I had clear intentions: I wanted to deepen my faith and relationship with God, be present physically and emotionally for my family, and align my work with my purpose. The last one felt like a monumental task. It was within that step of faith that God began to move and reveal Himself within my life. Without the chaotic schedule and brain burnout that had been my constant state of being, I began to seek and sense Him more than ever. It was a bold and scary move, but it set the wheels in motion for true healing to begin.

I gave God my full attention. For the first time, He was front and center in my life. I began to pray and read Scripture regularly, and seek guidance from God in everything. I was clear with God about my heart's desires, and I needed Him to be evident and apparent to me in response, and I told him so.

I continued to reflect on this idea of purpose. I prayed, "God, whatever my next career move is, I want to know without an ounce of doubt that I am walking in my purpose and Your will for my life." One morning, as I studied my Bible, I came across "The Great Commission." In this scripture, Jesus has just risen from the dead and, seeing his disciples for the first time since His resurrection, He tells them:

> *All authority in heaven and on earth has been given to me.*
> *Therefore, go and make disciples of all nations, baptizing them*
> *in the name of the Father and of the Son and of the Holy Spirit,*
> *and teaching them to obey everything I have commanded you.*
> *And surely I am with you always, to the very end of the age.*
> *– Matthew 28:18-20 (NIV)*

OH... THAT! I thought to myself. Of course: God has commanded us each to share the good news of salvation with everyone. Coming into this realization, my prayer became, "But how, God? How can I align my work with Your purpose for my life?"

Then it happened. I began to think more and more about my childhood and the things that had happened to me when I was young. *Oh boy! That's big.* I started to realize that my purpose had been there all along. I had always known I would share my story with the world someday; what I didn't know was that the time had come.

It was January of 2018. I had been on my "break from work" for six months and had been going on several interviews both in the private and public sectors, each time I left the room feeling drained and insecure. The opportunities I was considering were exciting, but I just didn't feel as though they would support my family life in the way that I needed. I didn't know which direction to take. I had applied for a leadership position at HOPE and was not selected. Helen Torres, the Executive Director, asked me during a debrief call what I wanted to pursue next, and I shared with her that I was feeling unsure of which direction to take. She suggested I talk to one of the leadership coaches they worked with, and I did. That's how I met Noelia, the woman who helped me explore my purpose and next steps for my career. On our first meeting together, she asked me this question, "If you could do anything in the world and money was no object, what would you do?" My response: "I would write a book about my life, focused on the challenges I overcame and how." It surprised me that this desire bubbled up to the surface instantly and without hesitation. I decided to pursue my lifelong goal of becoming an author. And so began our experiment. I decided I would begin by writing a blog and telling the world what happened. I began writing about the abuse I had experienced and what God has done in my life. The day I wrote that first post, in which I shared with the world that I had been a victim of childhood sexual abuse, there was a thrill and excitement that I cannot fully describe. I knew in that moment, that was what I was meant to do. It's amazing what can happen when others believe in us. These women believed in me before I knew how to truly believe in myself, and when I finally brought God into all of it, what happened was miraculous: I began to soar.

That day I knew this was my purpose and I was going to move forward with vulnerability and honesty. If you are interested in learning more about the role of vulnerability in healing, I highly recommend you read Dr. Brown's book, *Rising Strong: How the Ability to Reset Transforms the Way We Live, Love, Parent, and Lead.*

But the excitement was short-lived. Fear quickly rose up within me and spiraled as I indulged it in my mind. So many questions ran through my mind.

Am I really going to tell the world my deepest, darkest secrets?
What will they say?
How will they see me?
Will they feel sorry for me?
Will they trust me around their children once they know I have this awful past?
Or worse, am I exposing my children to the very danger I want to protect them from by stepping into this work?

This became my biggest fear. Not only did I indulge it and allow it to gain momentum, but I sat in it for weeks, trying to decide what to do, how much to say, and if I would ever post the piece I had written at all. I deleted the details and rewrote it numerous times. I had other fears too. I knew it would take time to write my story and get it out into the market. Publishing it would require a significant investment, and at the time I wasn't sure how we were going to fund my project. I also felt inadequate and inexperienced within this field. I thought to myself, "I am not a psychologist. Who am I to tell the world with any degree of certainty what they could do to improve their lives? Finally, what difference could I possibly make anyway?" Fear is a powerful thing, it has the power to keep us stuck in a bad situation, stifling our purpose and our potential. *That fear is how I knew I had to do this. I knew that if I felt this afraid, then I was on the verge of something big and important. I chose to press on and pressed "Post."* If you are interested in learning more about how to identify and address fear, I suggest Tara Mohr's book *Playing Big: Practical Wisdom for Women Who Want to Speak Up, Create, and Lead,* for further study.

Once something is out in the atmosphere, it has a way of taking a life of its own. The comments and direct messages started pouring in. Friends and acquaintances I had known for years stepped forward and said, "That happened to me too." They proceeded to tell me how brave I was and how much they admired my courage. A close friend even said, "I have yet to find the courage to speak my truth. Thank you!" In the weeks that followed, it seemed everywhere I went, someone had seen my post, read my story, and wanted to talk. I listened to story after story about how a cousin, family friend, uncle, church leader, and even fathers had robbed their children of the joy and innocence of their childhood. In many cases, they had never told anyone before or they had said something but had not been believed or heard—I mean really heard—in the way they desperately needed, and didn't even know it. I recognized that, with my voice, I provided a safe space for them to speak their own experiences. I recognized in that moment that I was giving voice not only to my struggles but to the hundreds of women (and men) who had yet to tell anyone their secret. So what difference could I possibly make? Perhaps all the difference, while, as an alternative, my continued silence would help no one. I prayed for purpose and God spoke to me, loud and clear.

Is there something in your life that you want to do but are too afraid to move in that direction? That something could change your life and the lives of others.

Fear may be fighting against something important that God wants to give you; something you are meant to do. The presence of fear is confirmation that you must act. The stronger the fear you feel, the more relevant the thing you are supposed to do.

God doesn't just want to set you free. He wants to call you into your purpose. You can choose to stay silent, but what if you are the one person who has the exact words that someone needs to hear so that God could transform their lives? I don't know where you are in your journey. Maybe you have kept your secret buried deep inside all these years. Maybe you told someone, and they neglected to respond and react in the way you needed—with compassion and outrage. Maybe you weren't believed. If that's your story, I'm so sorry and I believe you. I want you to know that you matter. Your experiences are important and you deserved better. Not only that; you are valuable and beautiful and one of a kind—as resilient as they come, by the way—because you are here taking steps to address your past and heal, truly.

There is still a lot that I don't know how He will provide, but I'm now living in a season in which I am called to rely on Him for *everything*, literally on a daily basis, and this has changed my life. My journey of healing challenged, triggered me, and called me to rely on God like never before. Each morning I begin with, "Okay God, what do you want me to do today? What do you want to say to Your children?"

Lean into God in all things; do not be afraid because He is with you and He has good things in store for you. He will not forsake you. You are reading this book because He loves you, He is extending His hand to reach for you. He knows that you were lonely, afraid, discouraged, and in a rut, and He wants to bring you out into a full life. Remember though, you're going to have to reach for it! He cannot force Himself on you. He will not—it is against His nature. You're going to have to make the choice; the choice lies within you. He did not bring you into this awareness to be afraid; He wants to protect you.

For God has not given us a spirit of fear and timidity,
but of power, love, and self-discipline.
2 Timothy 1:7 (NLT)

Part Two

HOW HE HEALED AND MADE ME NEW

INVITING HEALING (DESIRE)

TRUSTING GOD (DEPEND)

CHOOSING TO WALK WITH GOD (DECIDE)

CHAPTER 10

What Does It Mean to Be a Christian?

E arly in my faith journey, I believed that being a Christian meant you had prayed "The Sinner's Prayer"—the prayer I had prayed when I was eight years old to accept Jesus into my heart. I also believed that Christians attended church regularly and lived according to all those rules I learned from the Christians I was around early in my faith. The truth is that someone who does all of those things has a religion. Being a Christian is so much more.

For years, I walked with an incomplete perspective of who God is, what He did for us when He sent His one and only Son to die on a cross for us, and the promises He holds for those of us who choose to walk with Him. In this section, I will walk you through how I invited in the healing that transformed me, what happened when I placed my trust in Him completely, and will clarify some misconceptions about what it means to walk with God.

When I left my career in government, I finally started to fully let God into my life. But what does that mean?

I learned growing up that salvation was something that needed to be earned. When I was first introduced to Jesus, I desperately yearned for a savior to rescue me out of the fear and confusion that dominated my life. But I thought I needed to earn salvation and that I would never reach it because I kept messing up.

I don't think this is unique to my experience. When we come to Jesus, we don't always have someone to guide us and teach us a solid foundation of what it means to be Christian. We form our perceptions of Christianity and, more importantly, of God based on what we see those around us live out as part of their faith. What we don't realize is that what we see is usually not a complete picture but rather a moment in their lives. We may see the fruits of the Spirit—love, joy, peace, patience, kindness, goodness, faithfulness, gentleness, and self-control (Galatians 5:23). These are certainly the "fruits of the Spirit," and by these characteristics you can recognize a true Christian. However, what we don't see are the internal struggles and battles they fight and therefore develop the idea that they are close to perfect and can do no wrong. This is an incorrect assumption. Even the strongest Christian has moments of weakness in which they slip and do not reflect the character of God.

We must understand first that our nature is imperfect. The Bible tells us "the flesh is weak," and, even after accepting Jesus into our heart as Lord and Savior, we will experience moments of weakness and at times give in to temptations and make mistakes (Matthew 26:41). God knew this from the beginning. He created us. That's exactly why He provided a way for us to go back to Him. His grace is such that regardless of those mistakes, He loves us and forgives us time and again. Do not misinterpret this as a free pass to do as you please. We have a forgiving, merciful Father in heaven who understands, but One who also requires obedience. I'll elaborate on this later. What I want you to understand is that you, too, must have grace for yourself as you reach for Him. You will make mistakes, and you must forgive yourself for your mistakes and continue to strive to live as Jesus taught and exemplified for us.

Or, on the flip-side, we may experience Christians on their weakest days when they can do nothing but misrepresent God. Many have seen the failures of professed Christians and given up on God altogether. They, too, deserve our grace. God is still working in them. They are not necessarily a fraud; they are just in a season of struggle. We all begin as babies in our faith, and, as such, we need proper nourishment and guidance in order to grow and mature in strength in our walk with God. It could be that that individual is still working out their struggles and has not yet developed the character that God will produce in them in time, if they continue to seek Him. Know that Christians are flawed human beings just like everyone else walking this earth. The difference between a Christian and a non-Christian is not visible. It is an invisible relationship with God and a posture on the inside—a posture that places more value on invisible and eternal things than on visible and temporary riches. I accepted Jesus into my life when I was eight years old. As you've read, I was sexually abused between the ages of five and ten years old. This left me with feelings I did not understand. As I shared earlier, I had a relationship with Him after all of that happened, but eventually I gave up feeling I would never be good enough.

I had a lot to work through, and early in my adult life, I made a conscious decision to walk away from Him. I thought I was better off without Him. I became angry and resentful toward Him. I didn't understand how a loving God could allow the terrible abuses that happen to innocent children. I blamed Him for the harm done to me by the evil choices of people close to me and launched into my season of rebellion. I was promiscuous, proud, and even questioned my sexual identity for a time. I was also selfish, I only cared about myself, what I wanted, needed, desired, and deserved. I will tell you more about my season of rebellion and questioning later.

Still, He never left me. Time and time again, He reached for me, placing people in my life that would tell me of Him and give me His love. I wanted nothing to do with those people and did all I could to avoid them. I didn't know it, but God was pursuing me, calling me back to Him. I couldn't hear Him because I didn't want to.

That selfishness was challenged once I became a wife and mother. My family was my saving grace. They were the gift that led me to realize that I needed to change. I knew I needed to heal and that only God could help me do that. I knew that if I continued to ignore Him, I had the potential to hurt my own family—the very people I wanted to protect. I was determined to give them a life that was completely different from the one I had growing up.

I finally turned to Him in surrender, knowing that only He could help me in the secret places of my mind that continued to be haunted by my past.

He not only forgave me, but He revealed all my brokenness to me and healed me in surprising ways. He has *transformed* me. Still, I struggle and make mistakes. I have days when I'm moody, less than kind, and still have trust issues I am working on, and more. He knows.

However, I've learned to see myself as God does. I am His no matter what, forgiven and living in His grace. He forgives the big and the small things as long as in my heart and mind I am genuinely seeking His will.

And some self-proclaimed "Christians" are doing anything but. The worst, I believe, comes when someone does harm to others while calling themselves a Christian, and on the inside, they are not at all trying to walk in righteousness; they are like wolves in sheep's clothing.

Beware of false prophets
who come disguised as harmless sheep
but are really vicious wolves.
– Matthew 7:15

If you have encountered this and experienced abuse as a result, my heart goes out to you. I hope that in this section I can clarify some things about what it means to follow Jesus genuinely and adequately describe God's nature versus our nature.

Whenever I speak with people who have turned away from God and want nothing to do with Him, they tell me stories of how people in the Church disappointed or hurt them. We have all heard about cases of abuse in the Church. This, I believe, is the most damaging form of abuse because it raises barriers between people and God himself. When we are hurt by our spiritual leaders, or people in our lives who claim to be Christians but do not live according to God's heart, it causes us to unfairly blame God for the actions of people who are actually far from Him. I pray that God will help me to show His true nature, grace, and love for you in a way that brings you into the understanding that God is not to blame for what has happened, and happens, to you in this life at the hands of people. I will cover in this section what a Christian looks like and what they do not. I will also discuss why Christians believe in the Bible, the power of choice, and the gift of free will God has given each one of us, and, ultimately, how you, too, can walk with God in a process that takes time but that you need not fear.

I don't know what you believe about Christianity. Perhaps like me, you also learned an incomplete perspective of faith and, therefore, of God. I am here to tell you all those man-made rules I mentioned earlier are not found anywhere in the Bible—and trust me, I've looked. Nowhere does it say, *Thou shalt not wear makeup, style your hair, wear pants, or listen to music*, etc. The only cut-and-dry list of rules I have found in the Bible is the one God revealed to Moses. We know this list as the Ten Commandments (Exodus 20:1-17).

God gave the people all these instructions:

1. *You must not have any other god but me.*
2. *You must not make for yourself an idol of any kind or an image of anything in the heavens or on the earth or in the sea.*
3. *You must not misuse the name of the Lord your God.*
4. *Remember to observe the Sabbath day by keeping it holy.*
5. *Honor your father and mother.*
6. *You must not murder.*
7. *You must not commit adultery.*
8. *You must not steal.*
9. *You must not testify falsely against your neighbor.*
10. *You must not covet your neighbor's house. You must not covet your neighbor's wife, male or female servant, ox or donkey, or anything else that belongs to your neighbor.*

These are important moral absolutes that everyone should follow. In fact, most of our laws are based in these as well.

It could also be that someone told you that certain behaviors were not "Christ-like." Perhaps, you too, experienced feeling that you would never be able to measure up to God's expectations when, in reality, those were man-made standards. I want you to know that God loves you exactly the way you are, and He does not expect you to live by an interpretation of His rules handed down to you by a flawed individual. This is exactly why it's important that we study the Bible.

These things happened to them as examples and were written down as warnings for us.
1 Corinthians 10:11 (NIV)

The standards you can aspire to live by are all in the *Holy Bible*. As Christians, we believe the Bible was inspired by God Himself. That is the book you can turn to in order to learn about what God expects of you. Not only that, but there you will learn who He is, who you are, and all the things He made for you because He loves you. I encourage you to dust off your Bible and read it. Ask God to give you eyes to see what He intended for you through the words written in it and to read it with the eyes of a student who desires to learn. There are many ways you can study the Bible. You can download a Bible application on your phone. There are many free versions that also have a wealth of Bible plans for any topic you want to learn about. Bible plans are a discussion of a variety of topics with scriptural references and a teaching that can be applied to your everyday life. These have helped me tremendously in my walk with God.

Perhaps you attempted to read the Bible in the past and found the language to be confusing or archaic. You should know that there are many translations of the Bible that maintain the intent and message of the Word but that have been translated into easy-to-understand, contemporary language. I personally really like the New

Living Translation (NLT). You will find I mostly quote the scripture throughout this book from this version, but you should take a look at several and see which translation resonates with you.

I encourage you to consider what you believe a *Christ follower* looks like and consider the source. Could it be that someone you saw as a Christian walked and talked a certain way, and you formed an idea of Christianity based on their behaviors and actions? I would caution you against forming your idea of Christianity solely on the behaviors of self-proclaimed Christians. Here is a little revelation I wish I had known long ago: A Christian is someone who believes that Jesus is the Son of God, and that He died and rose again. Further, a Christ-follower is someone who studies the Word of God—the Bible—for the purpose of learning about God. A Christian is someone who aspires to become more like Jesus by applying what they learn in the Bible to their lives. A Christian is not someone who perfectly lives by a set of man-made rules. Whoever you learned from, they are not perfect and not necessarily who you should model yourself after if you seek to please God. A Christian is a mother, a daughter, a friend, a colleague, a neighbor—and she is not perfect! The biggest danger I see in modeling your faith after the actions of imperfect human beings is that they are likely to disappoint you.

My pastor who taught me to pray, taught me the rules to follow as a Christian, and inspired me to sing and even teach the word of God when I was only a child, appeared to make some grave mistakes in his walk with God. I was too young to fully comprehend what happened at the time; I was only privy to overhearing conversations among adults in my family who attended the same church, but it was rumored that he had attempted to have an affair with a member of our church. This incident, whether it was rumor or truth, ultimately lost him his reputation, his congregation, his career, and even his marriage. Many members of our church turned away from their faith due to disappointment, and the church eventually disbanded and disappeared. I caution you on this front, and urge you to look to the Bible to find the truth about what it means to follow Jesus. Further, you can look to Jesus if you want to know what it means to be a Christian or Christ follower. Jesus Christ is the Son of God, and was the only man to ever walk a sinless life.

We, as humans, cannot live a sinless life. We will continue to struggle, make mistakes, and even disappoint one another on occasion, but the more we look to Jesus as the model for our lives and example of how we should treat one another, the less likely we are to make grave mistakes that cause our lives or relationships to crumble.

Before I chose to return to an actual church building and made a commitment to be an active member of a community of Christians, my speakers were my church. I'd listen to church podcasts in my car during my commute to work. God began to grow my faith, just like that, Him and I, through my phone in my car. So if you have been let down by the church, and by that I mean disappointed or hurt by His people, know that we are all sinners with high potential for good and evil—all of us. None of us are perfect. We aren't always the best representatives of God. I'm sorry that happened to you. And I get it. Always remember there are other ways to connect with God.

If church is not for you, or if you are not a fan of organized religion, you can begin by praying and listening to great podcasts and beginning a relationship with Jesus this way. Eventually, I hope that you will choose to take the step to start to trust His people, while always remembering that we are all human and imperfect. There are great Bible teachers in local churches. The physical church is a place to learn more about the Word of God, to worship, and to connect with other Christians. We are stronger together, and within relationships we can help each other grow in our walk with God. It is in relationships with people that we help one another grow both in faith and in everyday life.

As iron sharpens iron, so a friend sharpens a friend.
— Proverbs 27:17 (NLT)

For now, you can listen to His message and be in conversation one-on-one with your Heavenly Father. You have access to great teachings from all over the world through your phone or computer. He sees and hears you, and you can learn and grow by meditating on the things of God in prayer, worship, Scripture, and through great podcasts.

Central to a Christian's life is prayer. Let's look deeper at this together next.

―――――――――――――― Contemplation ――――――――――――――

Here, I want to take a moment to check-in on you. We've covered a lot. How are you doing? In your journal, write the answers to the following questions underneath the words *Desire, Depend,* and *Decide.*

Desire – What questions are coming up for you as you read? What do you want to know, heal, or change?

Depend – Is there something you read in this section about relying on God that you would like to bring forward with you? Is there anything you are wrestling with God about?

Decide – What are you going to *do* differently in this area going forward?

Journal your thoughts. We'll come back to these later.

CHAPTER 11
Worship and the Power of Prayer

W orship was always my favorite part of service as a young Christian. There are many ways to worship God, among them service to our family, our communities, and our professions. Prayer, worship, and Bible study are not only a form of honoring God, but they are also a form of communication between us and our Creator.

Worship is one of the best ways to calm and quiet an anxious mind. Worship keeps my mind from wandering and revisiting memories that drain me of joy. I love to focus on the all-powerful God who holds my hand in every instance. There is a peace and comfort that washes over me when I fill the air and my mind with melodic prayers of worship and love unto God. This has always been a bridge between me and God.

No matter what is happening in my life, worship music calms me and focuses me on what truly matters. I play it every moment I can. It is powerful—it silences my anxious thoughts and elevates me to Heaven. When I first heard the song "Set a Fire" by Jesus Culture, I was propelled into a deeper and more intimate relationship with God. I sang out completely honestly, "I want more of you, God." This is where the deepening of my relationship with God started. I wanted to feel that burning fire for Him that the lyrics spoke about. "The Garden" by Kari Jobe reminded me that God can turn pain into power, brokenness into wholeheartedness, weakness into strength, and my life into beauty. I related to lyrics from her song: "I had all but given up, desperate for a sign from God" when I was considering leaving my career in government. The song *Oceans* by Hillsong United literally gave me the courage to step out into the unknown when I quit my job to pursue a deeper relationship with Him and to know His purpose for my life. I went back to that song countless times when I felt like I was losing my nerve to move forward into uncertain territory. Deciding to tell the world my story and help women heal childhood sexual abuse was very new for me. He was transforming my heart and mind—completing a work in me from self-centeredness to having an outer focus: "The Cause of Christ." Today, the song on repeat in my car is Hillsong United's "Who You Say I Am." This has been the soundtrack to my healing journey. These worship songs helped me to connect with God and remain in a state of prayer.

When you first become a Christian, it can feel awkward and embarrassing to sing out. As you begin to mature, worship becomes a prayer and request to God that you receive what is being sung out.

There came a point in my spiritual walk when I realized that my heart had been transformed, and the worship songs held a new meaning. My heart was no longer asking to feel the freedom we professed through these songs. My heart was rejoicing, and I was in the freedom of my healing. I sang out, "I Am Who You Say I Am." The freedom I spoke of with my words was coming not from a heart that desperately wanted it, but from one that was walking in it. I had made it to the other side and was reveling in the light of my Creator fully. I no longer sing in request, desiring to feel the words truly. I sing from a place of victory: "I am who He says I am!" I feel it in my bones; He is with me; I am His; I am truly victorious.

If you struggle with fear or anxiety, meditate . . . *on Him*. Worship has done a lot for my faith and relationship with God. When done with a focused and open heart, it is like a sweet aroma that rises up to heaven. Worship is a powerful prayer that will transcend your situation and circumstances and elevate you into the presence of God. You will know you are in His presence because the feeling is unlike anything you've ever felt: the warmth . . . the comfort . . . the peace . . . the depths of which can sometimes only be expressed through tears and chills throughout your body. You may not have the words to speak the deepest truths of your heart, but your Creator programmed you to both recognize and respond when you seek that space willingly with a hunger to receive. This is when you will experience true breakthrough and pivots in your life that will propel you into who He created you to be.

In this second section of the book, I want to stir in you some conversations with your Heavenly Father.

The Lord says I was ready to respond but no one asked for help.
I was ready to be found but no one was looking for me.
I said here I am, here I am, to a nation that did not call my name.
All day long I opened my arms . . .
– Isaiah 65:1-7

Healing: God is the answer...and the conversation starts in prayer

If you want to see God's power moving in your life, ask of Him according to His will as reflected in His Word. The world can only work as God intended when we walk by faith and seek to follow the blueprint. Doing this in my life has been miraculous.

When I was a child, I prayed a bold prayer: "Don't ever let me go, even if I turn away from you. Don't ever leave me." He never did. An amazing thing happens when we pray according to God's will. Heaven pours down on us. Nothing pleases God more than when our heart is in alignment with His. It is that alignment that allows us to walk in His promises.

Years passed before I understood that the key to knowing who God is stands within the pages of the Holy Bible. We cannot know His will unless we study the written Word He left for us. The Bible is our manual to all of life's struggles. Once you read it and apply it to your life, even when it's hard and uncomfortable, His promises will manifest in your life in miraculous ways. I tell you this with full confidence because I lived it. He doesn't hold back His love based on external things. He looks at the heart within us. Our secret thoughts and desires are what connects or separates us from God.

Jesus' ministry on earth was one of mercy and kindness. He showed kindness to women caught in adultery, prostitutes, and lepers. They captured His heart, and when they reached for Him with faith, He healed, forgave, and cleansed them. In John 8:11, Jesus helps a woman caught in adultery. He tells the mob who is ready to stone her to death, "Let the one who has never sinned throw the first stone!" Not one condemned her because they knew in their hearts none were sinless. Jesus is then quoted saying, "Go and sin no more." This matters to Him.

However, you don't need to be perfected first before you reach for Him. He loves you exactly as you are. The gospel of Jesus Christ shows us that while we are flawed and selfish, God loves us so completely that He chose to pay the price for our transgressions. The payment for sin is death. He chose to take that payment upon Himself by becoming a man and settling our debt, so that we could have eternal life beyond the grave (John 3:16). That is the "Good News" I want to share with you, with the honest truth of my life. I know you can relate to my struggles. It's the reason why I decided to be vulnerable and tell you where I came from and what happened to me when I was a child. This is important because until you understand the magnitude and power of His Word, you cannot fully embrace and receive Him. I hope to tell you in terms you can relate to by sharing my truths. I want you to know where I've been and what I've done and who I am today—and more importantly *whose* I am. Because, if God can heal, forgive, and make me brand new, He certainly can do the same for you. I had heard this Good News many times. I had accepted Jesus, too, but until I understood the magnitude, permanence, and power of His sacrifice on the cross (Hebrews 10), I remained striving to earn His love, salvation, and still carrying the weight of my sin and struggles.

This same Good News that came to you
is going out all over the world.
It is bearing fruit everywhere by changing lives, just as
it changed your lives from the day you first heard and
understood the truth about God's wonderful grace.
– Colossians 1:6 (NLT)

THE VOICE OF GOD

One of the first things I realized as I prayed for *clarity of purpose* was that the Bible calls us to share the Gospel with our friends and neighbors. Of course, I thought, our mission as Christians is to share the good news of forgiveness and salvation (ESV John 3:16-18). "But how, God?" I continued to pray.

God started to make Himself very clear.

One morning, I returned from volunteering in my daughter's classroom with a nasty migraine. I closed the drapes in my room and lay down, hoping to soothe my head and eyes. I was unable to sleep because my dogs were going nuts barking. I got up, angry and ready to yell at my little Chanel and Rocky. When I got to the kitchen, I thought with frustration, *What are you guys barking at?*

As those words crossed my mind, I heard the sound of a male voice. It was an older man with confidence and authority. He simply said my name: "Karla!"

Naturally, I responded, asking, "Yeeesss?" I was alone with my dogs and thought, *Oh, I know what's going on—my kitchen window is open and someone must have been ringing my door bell. That's what all the barking is about.* I looked through my blinds to discover my window wasn't open. I checked my front door. No one was there. *Okay . . . now what?*

I had been praying for some time, asking, "God, speak to me. I'm going to need you to be really clear with me if I am going to hear you."

Well, the last thing I expected was an actual audible voice to emerge out of thin air.

As you can imagine, I felt afraid. I immediately thought, *Whatever that was, I guess it's time to pray.* I got on my knees and proceeded to pray. I went to God with my fear. "I'm afraid God—what is happening here?" I proceeded to read my Bible for a while. Nothing else odd happened that morning, thank goodness! I don't know how I would have handled it. I wondered, "Was something good or bad calling my name?" In fact, I couldn't be alone in my kitchen for two days after that. But I realized, God has not given me a spirit of fear.

> *For God has not given us a spirit of fear and timidity,*
> *but of power, love and self-discipline.*
> *– 2 Timothy 1:7 (NLT)*

I kept repeating that verse in the days that followed, and it brought me peace.

Whatever it was, that moment caused me to dive deeper into my faith. There is a real and invisible world in the atmosphere that we do not perceive with our human eyes or ears, usually (Ephesians 6:12, ESV). In the end, I resolved that it was in fact the voice of God, or an angel, and I started to trust fully in God's protection over my family. I know this now because that moment caused me to dive deeper into trusting Him.

I have begun to hear the voice of God more and more clearly since then, not in the audible way I did that one mysterious morning while I was alone in my kitchen, but within my consciousness through what I call divine inspiration and the wise counsel of those who love me.

Have you ever wondered what people mean when they speak of "the voice of God"? What does that mean? How does one know a thought is not our own, but inspired by the one, true God? How do we know He has called us to change or act? The voice of God is not usually audible, but is rather like a nudging sensation, an urge to say or do something.

It can be subtle. Some call it a gut feeling, a sixth sense, or intuition. It's that thought that crosses your mind, and you get the feeling you should listen. At times, you may ignore it and think later, *I should have listened to my intuition!* We all have an intuition about us that protects us from potentially harmful situations or encourages us to be braver than we are comfortable, but the voice of God is different in that it sets us on the correct path and encourages us to do only what is good for us.

His direction also comes as internal conflict and tension you can physically feel in your stomach, neck, or chest. That type of pressure is usually highlighting something that isn't working as it should be. For example, you may have experienced internal conflict in a job that isn't meeting your personal needs, an unhealthy relationship, or a situation in which things just aren't going right. No matter what you do, you are hitting a wall and ending up in the space of dissatisfaction. Friend, that is the voice of God or the Holy Spirit. That tension you feel is God redirecting you.

You know a thought is not your own but divine inspiration because the nudge or tension you feel is calling you to step outside of your comfort zone, do something bold and scary, and behave in radically different ways than you have in the past. When you listen, you get confirmation pretty quickly, because there is a feeling of comfort, certainty, and assurance—a sense of peace within. Even if it was difficult, you feel right about the choice or decision you made.

Further, when He calls you to do something new, bold, or scary, He makes a way for you. Doors begin to open. Connections are made; things start to line up and move you forward. This cannot happen, though, until you step out and obediently follow the instruction you are sensing. When you do, then He delivers. This was the case for me when I made the decision to say yes to God when He revealed my purpose.

That's how you know you are walking in *your purpose*, His Will for you. It feels like pure heavenly intervention from above. I was at HOPE's annual Latina History Day conference in Los Angeles one evening, attending a panel discussion on sexual harassment in the workplace centered around the #MeToo movement, and noticed that not one person mentioned childhood sexual abuse. I knew what I had experienced in the places where I had worked and wanted to tell them that I believe the current workplace sexual abuse crisis is yet another devastating effect of childhood sexual abuse. I didn't have the courage to speak up. At the time, I had only shared my story with a few people close to me. I had not yet told the world what had happened to me when I was only five years old. I had only recently decided I would write my book.

I was also in this very gray area where I didn't even know how to introduce myself. My identity had always been connected to the organizations where I worked. This had been on my mind all night: "How will I introduce myself?" I was used to handing someone a business card and confidently identifying myself by my work. Conversations were easy in a professional setting because my identity was in my work, and I really didn't have to tell anyone anything about who I really was. I found myself completely unattached and exploring my purpose, considering entrepreneurship, redefining who I was as a professional and what I wanted to give my energy to.

That night, recognizing the obvious gap in the conversation, I made the bold decision to begin to speak my truth and, further, I decided to share that I was writing a book on healing childhood sexual abuse with the help of God. After the event ended, I noticed a group of women huddled on stage praying. The group included several of the speakers and women in the audience. I knew instantly that I wanted to meet them. I walked to the front of the room, extended my hand, and began to connect with the ladies. Immediately, I was asked the dreaded question, "What do you do?" I decided to share with the ladies that I was a survivor of childhood sexual abuse and was writing a book on healing. That was the moment it happened; I had said yes to God and voiced it to the world.

Have you ever heard anyone say that once you speak something out with your words, the universe conspires to bring it to fruition? This couldn't be more true. One of the ladies nearby, who had also been praying with the group, turned to me and asked me to tell her more. She proceeded to tell me she felt the Holy Spirit saying to her that she needed to support me and offered to mentor me. She told me she knew I had an important message to share with the world, and she was going to help me. It turns out the woman who graciously offered to support me after knowing me for all of two minutes is Dr. Betty Uribe, a published author and the Vice President of California Bank and Trust. She was also our keynote speaker during breakfast the following day of the conference. Imagine my shock and surprise. An international executive and Latina leader believed in me instantly—this was inspiring and motivating.

In the following weeks, Dr. Uribe connected me with the wonderful people who helped me make my dream a reality. I sensed the voice of God, as did she, and made the choice to respond in obedience. Since that moment, I have witnessed miracle after miracle as God led me to the exact contacts and resources I needed to launch into this new and exciting area of work in which I seek to empower women and lead them to God's healing. The Holy Spirit is a gift from God that allows us to see and think in new ways. The Bible tells us that we receive the Holy Spirit when we accept Jesus as our Lord and Savior.

Repent and be baptized, every one of you, in the name of Jesus Christ for the forgiveness of your sins. And you will receive the gift of the Holy Spirit.
— Acts 2:38 (NIV)

When we draw near to God, He comes near to us (James 4:8, ESV). The more you seek His voice, the more you can discern it. As you deepen your relationship with God, you will grow in wisdom and begin to see more clearly the things that bring you closer to Him and those that make you feel separated from Him. He will guide your path. Trust Him and get to know Him.

This is important because we can get misled by things that appear attractive and good but, in reality, leave us empty and dissatisfied time and again. I spent years pursuing professional and financial success, and romantic relationships to fill the void I felt in my life. I was always chasing something or someone, thinking that the next thing would be the thing to make me happy, but it never did. I invite you to listen more closely to the tone of the voice in your head. Is it God speaking to you, or someone else?

The voice of God is a small and gentle voice. If you're unsure, try this: Ask Him something and then just sit and listen for the first thing that crosses your mind. He will answer, with one or just a few words sometimes that carry a powerful message. I once asked God something very specific, and in just a couple of words, He told me exactly what I needed to know and do to fix the problem I was contemplating. Our conversation went like this: "God, what am I going to do about my marriage? There is a distance between us that I can't seem to cross. I feel as though a brick wall has been erected between us. I don't know if I put it there or if he [my husband] did, but I can't seem to get through to the other side. What can I do to bridge that distance or get over that wall?"

Here is exactly what came to me in a second: "Humble yourself, and I will heal your marriage."

Of course! I was astonished. Next, I remembered a specific verse in the Bible that tells us, if we would humble ourselves and turn from our wicked ways, He will heal our land.

Here is the exact verse:

If My people who are called by My name
put away their pride and pray,
and look for My face, and turn from their sinful ways,
then I will hear from heaven. I will forgive
their sin, and will heal their land.
– 2 Chronicles 7:14 (NLV)

That "if and then" statement is a promise. IF we do this THEN He will respond in a specific way. God was not only telling me how to solve our problem, He also told me where to find further instruction in the Bible. This is a very important detail I cannot neglect to share with you. His voice NEVER contradicts the instructions He already left for us in the physical Bible. Any question you have about relationships, purity, money, and life, you can find answers for in the Bible. The more you study the Bible, the more He will speak to you through it, and the more it will speak into your life when you are searching for answers.

As far as the dialogue in your head, this is how you can clearly recognize the voice of God. God is Love.

And love is patient and kind. Love is not jealous or boastful or proud or rude. It does not demand its own way. It is not irritable, and it keeps no record of being wronged. It does not rejoice about injustice but rejoices whenever the truth wins out. Love never gives up, never loses faith, is always hopeful, and endures through every circumstance.
—1 Corinthians 13:4-7 (NLT)

Any thought that rises up in your mind that doesn't reflect these characteristics IS NOT God's voice. More often than not, the voice in our head is not a nice one. We tend to be really harsh with ourselves. You can be sure that that voice is NOT the voice of God. The voice of God isn't hypercritical, accusing, or condemning. It doesn't judge you, cut you down, or make you feel awful about yourself. It doesn't scare you to the point of keeping you stuck where you are. It doesn't rationalize that the bad you do is actually good. It doesn't insult others in secret.

It doesn't tell you to stay silent for fear of shame, ridicule, or error. All those insecurities in your head, those are not the voice of God. Those are the lies this world has fed you and some that you have invited through your behaviors and choices. You can choose to reject those thoughts by saying, "I reject that thought in the name of Jesus."

Learn to identify and silence the lies in your head by speaking truth over them. The Bible is full of truths about who you are and whose you are. Read the Word. Invite Jesus in and watch the dialogue in your head begin to change.

God's voice is gentle, patient, and kind.

In the darkest season of my life, the voice in my head was angry. I had this anger-fueled speak screaming in my head around the clock constantly, directed at strangers, at family . . . I couldn't even silence it during sex. I was consumed by lust and selfishness; only my needs mattered, and when I didn't have things my way, the monster inside me cursed at everything and everyone. I was constantly in a fight with someone: a boyfriend, a girlfriend, a stranger, my mother, my siblings.

He always speaks to me when I am alone, so it's no surprise that I heard that awful voice clearly for what it was when I was in my car driving. *Wow.* I realized that the "road rage" inside was deafening. *Hmm. Why am I angry all the time?* I began to notice the lines between my brows deepening; I was scowling all the time and I didn't know it, even when passersby said to me, "Smile, you're too pretty to be so mad."

"What?" I laughed it off and gave a forced smile. Meanwhile, I cursed at them on the inside.

The words that come out of our mouths are a product of that which is in our hearts, and I was in a season of shameless rebellion, in which I had given over to all my sinful desires, and hate was what poured out of me. Surprisingly, I didn't think much about my abuse in this season. I was distracted and destructive. I was not a kind person. I was not patient or gentle. I prided myself in being "straight out," "direct," "real," a "bitch"—yes, I said all those things out loud. I boasted in them.

The lies in your head do not come from God. They come from another invisible being, one you should run to God for shelter from.

There is no truth in him.
When he lies, he speaks his native language,
for he is a liar and the father of lies.
– John 8:44 (NIV)

If you truly seek God's voice, He will reveal Himself to you more and more.

The more I seek Him, the more I receive, and the stronger my faith muscles are becoming. His voice comes to me in whispers I know are not my own. I know the thoughts I'm having are not mine but divine inspiration because they address something I have been thinking about without clear direction of what to do. He quiets my fears, answers my questions, and brings peace where there was once doubt. When He directs me, I feel it right between my chest. The voice of God is how I arrived at my decision to write a book on abuse and His redeeming power. For more on how to hear the voice of God, I recommend *Whisper* by Mark Batterson.[7]

TALKING TO GOD

Before I turned my life over to God, I really doubted the power of prayer. I wondered, "Well, if everything is written and pre-ordained, then what's the point?"

I didn't understand that there are forces beyond our control, and not visible to the naked eye, that have an influence in our lives. One thing I learned when I began praying and reading the Word of God is that it has the power to change the atmosphere around us.

I struggled in the season that I was determined to get closer to God through prayer. There were moments when I would get closer to Him, and then I would become really afraid about different things. It was as if a battle was going on in my head fighting for space, seeking to dominate me, good versus evil. I told a friend about my internal struggle, and he advised me to do a Bible study on fear. He suggested I copy several scriptures that address fear, and whenever I felt afraid, to recite them. I did, and let me tell you: My fear vanishes instantly now. There is a peace that comes over me that I can only try to articulate.

Prayer works, friend. The Word of God is *alive*. It is powerful and it was left for us as a tool we can use not only to instruct us in how to live

---

[7] Batterson, Mark. *Whisper: How to Hear the Voice of God.* United States of America: Multnomah, 2017.

our lives, but also as a weapon to protect us in the invisible fight over our souls and against the many struggles we experience in this world.

TAKING STEPS IN FAITH

There may be some things you want and need, and have possibly even asked God for, and you are still waiting for a resolution and a response. I don't want you to think that because you are in a season of waiting that God is not as powerful as He says He is. The reason I believe my prayers have been answered quickly in certain seasons is because I asked and asked for a time, but also took steps in faith toward their fulfillment. When we ask and sit back and wait for God to do all of it for us, nothing happens. Before I left my career in government, I was thinking of leaving it for a long time—years even—but I didn't take any steps in that direction, even though I deeply desired a change. I was afraid that as a family we wouldn't be able to sustain the lifestyle we were used to. Faith requires courage and action. When we courageously move forward into the good things that we want for our lives, and trust that God will do what He has said He will do in the Bible, He will carry us through to the best outcome for us, and *that's* when we will see Him move in our lives.

Faith is about trusting in something without seeing. The Bible says God rewards those who believe without seeing.

*Now faith is confidence in what we hope for and
assurance about what we do not see.*
– Hebrews 11:1 (NIV)

Because of my past, I think I might always struggle with parental relationships. As you now know, I grew up in a home that was dysfunctional, explosive, and not very loyal. People looked out for their own interests and were distracted by the chaos they created. I wasn't born into a family I could turn to for advice, guidance, or leadership. I've begun to see Jesus as a big brother I can look up to. Our Heavenly

Father is my Creator and my King; but seeing Him as an older brother is easier for me. It helps me talk to Him.

My mother and biological father had two children, my brother Fred and I. Each of them made a new life after they divorced. My mother married my stepfather and together they had two children, my siblings Julio and Diana. My biological father is married to a wonderful lady. She overcame the tumultuous years of my father's rage. In his words, "She withstood the hurricane." Together they had five children, my siblings Jennifer, Andrea, Carlos, Kevin, and Jeffrey. I am the oldest sibling of nine children combined from my two sets of parents—five on my biological father's side and four of us including me on my mother's side. Because I'm the oldest, I never had an older brother who had an opportunity to hurt me, disappoint me, disrespect me, abuse me, or withhold his love. It makes sense to me that Jesus started to feel like an older brother. I sense Him in the room with me always, ever-present, ever loving, and consistent. His eyes are full of kindness and His arms outstretched, warm and welcoming. He is a wealth of love, wisdom, and encouragement. I can turn to Him and talk to Him openly and honestly. He never turns His back on me. I trust Him, welcome His presence and comfort. I feel safe in His presence.

Jesus asked, "Who is my mother? Who are my brothers?"
Then he pointed to his disciples and said, "Look, these are
my mother and brothers. Anyone who does the will of my
Father in heaven is my brother and sister and mother!"
– Matthew 12:48-50

I don't know who hurt you, but if you struggle with the idea of a Heavenly Father because your earthly father let you down, I encourage you to consider this scripture. God is so loving and so flexible. He invites you to become a part of His family, and He is not concerned with titles. He loves you unconditionally and welcomes you with open arms, regardless of whether you call Him Father or brother.

——————— Contemplation ———————

In your journal, write the answers to the following questions underneath the words *Desire, Depend,* and *Decide.*

Desire – What do you want to know, heal, or change?
Depend – Is there something you read in this section about relying on God that you would like to bring forward with you?
Decide – What are you going to *do* differently in this area going forward?

Journal your thoughts.

What questions are coming up for you as you read?

Is there anything you are wrestling with God about?

CHAPTER 12
Trust God's Promises

Blessed is she who has believed that the Lord
would fulfill his promises to her!
– Luke 1:45

SPIRITUAL WARFARE ─────────────────────────

C hild abuse is a powerful tool the enemy uses to effectively destroy lives. The Bible tells us the devil is crafty and full of strategies (Ephesians 6:11). "Trap them young, and they'll live a life of bondage" is the strategy where child abuse is concerned. Certainly, when a child is introduced to darkness at such a vulnerable and innocent age, they are set up to live life in a state of confusion. This was the case with me. My childhood was a nightmare. No one deserves such a tragic beginning.

When I decided to step into this work of helping people heal from childhood sexual abuse, I knew I was in for the fight of my life. I was going to unleash war on the darkness that had gripped me since I was five years old. I now know that God has a call on my life—that He wants to use me to bring light into the darkest corners of my being and others. I clearly saw His hand at work in me as I walked through the shut doors and dark hallways of my mind that had terrorized me my entire life. I prayed for space, time, clarity, and purpose seeking His will fully in every area of my life.

I had never been more terrified of doing anything in my adult life than I was the moment I knew God was calling me into battle, but creating something beautiful out of the rubble of devastation this life leaves in our hearts is something only He can bring about. While He did not create me for the experiences of my childhood, He knew they would happen, because of human nature. Yet He was with me all along, pursuing me, offering me His hand, his refuge. I was too angry to take it for years. When I finally did, He gripped my hand, enveloped me in His love and comfort, gave me new eyes to see (John 9:25), and walked me boldly into my purpose. I could never have let go of the anger myself, or brought down the walls that were built around me, keeping me from experiencing trust and loving relationships with others. He mended my broken heart, gave me a purpose, and healed me. It is through the visible transformation in the lives of His children that He demonstrates His power. I have experienced the radical transformation of my life, and I simply cannot keep it to myself. I want you to know what I experienced unfairly at the hands of the people who hurt me. I want to tell you about the bad choices I made as a result and what He did for me when I gave my life to Him. Because if He forgave, cleansed, and healed me, He will certainly do the same for you if you ask Him to. He is reaching for you. His hand doesn't get tired. He will keep holding it out, waiting for you. He is not one to give up on His children. Will you extend your hand, reach for Him, and let Him do for you what He has done for me? Perhaps even grander things He has planned for you.

"For I know the plans I have for you," says the Lord.
"They are plans for good and not for disaster, to
give you a future and a hope."
— Jeremiah 29:11

Sharing my deepest and most painful memories placed me in a very vulnerable position. I had concerns about how my truth would impact my children, husband, mother, father, and siblings. I worried about hurting and exposing stories that were not mine to tell. God led me in this direction, and I knew that anything I did with God firmly at the center would be good and hugely impactful.

Regardless of where you stand in your faith, we can all agree that childhood sexual abuse is evil. The Bible tells us we do not fight against flesh and blood but against the evil forces that dwell in the spiritual realm (Ephesians 6:12). Evil caused your abuser to do the things they did. This is also why I believe only God can deliver true healing. We have an enemy who comes to try to steal, kill, and destroy, but Jesus has come to give us a full and beautiful life (John 10:10). I told you before about how I accepted Jesus into my heart when I was eight years old, but I gave my life to Him when I was thirty-eight—that is *thirty years later*. Within those three decades, I struggled to follow Him without truly knowing Him and eventually gave up and turned from Him. It wasn't until I finally made the decision to surrender my life to Him and to walk in obedience that He really flooded in and transformed every part of me. Within the last year, God has been fulfilling His promises of healing in my life, not because he didn't want to or couldn't do it sooner, but because I wasn't ready to reflect honestly on my experiences, feel the feelings I had, grieve what I lost, and ask Him to heal me. He led me to this moment with a plan: To bring me through and out of the darkness.

PROMISES OF HEALING AND REDEMPTION ————

If My people who are called by My name
put away their pride and pray,
and look for My face, and turn from their sinful ways,
then I will hear from heaven. I will forgive
their sin, and will heal their land.
– 2 Chronicles, 7:14 (NLV)

Again, what a beautiful promise we have. What stands out to me the most in this scripture is that accepting that we alone do not have the power to heal the deep wounds of our past takes humility. Pride can be a tremendous barrier to overcome; pride separates us from God and from others. For a long time, I looked down at people who had less than me or knew less than me, not realizing that it was pride. This heart disposition was affecting all of my relationships.

God gives us the tools. When we seek Him in prayer, we will receive. He will forgive us and restore our land. Today, I stand firmly on this promise, and I know it's true because of the beautiful changes I experienced as a result of seeking Him. It has manifested in my life in several ways.

The Bible tells us that when we confess our sins, He forgives us and purifies us (1 John 1:9). Further, it tells us He will cast our sins as far from us as the East is from the West; He is slow to anger and loves us as a father loves his children (Psalms 103). You can trust Him. If you believe Jesus is the Son of God and confess it with your mouth and ask Him to be your Lord and Savior, He will forgive you, cleanse you of all the bad things that happened to you and the sinful choices you made as a result. He will send your transgressions as far as the East is from the West, where they cannot harm you anymore. If you have children, you know that the love of a parent is intense, strong, and unshakeable. I didn't understand that until I had children of my own, because as I shared with you, I didn't experience that type of love from my father or even my stepfather. Now that I am a mother, I understand the kind of love God has for us, because of how strongly I love my daughters.

If you confess with your mouth that Jesus is Lord and
believe in your heart that God raised him
from the dead, you will be saved.
For with the heart one believes and is justified, and
with the mouth one confesses and is saved.
– Romans 10:9-10 (ESV)

There it is—the key to your healing is answering the call of Jesus, and whom the Son sets free is free indeed (John 8:36). If you boldly take this step of faith, you will be free, claim it, own it, and live it out, and watch Him transform everything about you. This can be difficult to understand. I marvel at the life I now have. It is undeniable. I am a different person.

*When Jesus spoke again to the people, he
said, "I am the light of the world.
Whoever follows me will never walk in darkness,
but will have the light of life."
John 8:12 (NIV)*

It's all there, who He is, what He requires of us, and the promises He has made for those who follow Him.

GOD MAKES EVERYTHING BEAUTIFUL

God is a man of His Word. He promised He would give us beauty for ashes.

*...to bestow on them a crown of beauty
instead of ashes,
the oil of joy
instead of mourning,
and a garment of praise
instead of a spirit of despair.
They will be called oaks of righteousness,
a planting of the Lord
for the display of his splendor.
- Isaiah 61:3 (NIV)*

——————————— Contemplation ———————————

In your journal, write the answers to the following questions underneath the words *Desire, Depend,* and *Decide.*

Desire – What do you want to know, heal, or change?
Depend – Is there something you read in this section about relying on God that you would like to bring forward with you?
Decide – What are you going to *do* differently in this area going forward?

Journal your thoughts.

What questions are coming up for you as you read?

Is there anything you are wrestling with God about?

CHAPTER 13

Revelation

B efore my healing, just one year ago, courage was not a word I would have used to describe myself. I was always fearful— of *everything*. In the past year, God transformed my fear into courage and my pain into power. Where there was darkness, there is now light. His love is so great that once I opened the door to my heart and let Him in, He flooded in, filled me, and began spilling out of me into all of my relationships. I had heard it said that "the truth will set you free" (John 8:32), but had not understood what that truly meant until I began reading Scripture with a hunger for life, knowledge, and freedom. Proclaiming God's Word over my life broke the chains I didn't know were binding me.

The strength I projected was not real; it was fabricated by me and motivated by fear. My strength was a defense mechanism meant to keep others at a safe distance from my children, and me, where they could not hurt us.

DISCOVERING MY TRIGGERS

My history of physical abuse made me a very fearful person and created buttons in me that would immediately trigger me into a panic.

For example, when my children would argue with each other, their elevated voices would cause a visceral response within me that I could not control. My chest would lock up, I wouldn't be able to breathe, and

I would lose control. I would find myself screaming at my kids because I needed the noise to simply stop. I didn't want to yell at them, but I didn't know how else to respond to the instant panic I felt inside as a response.

My husband had to be very gentle with me for many years because his voice triggered me. He's a man, and his voice is deep and loud. He's also a strong guy who tends to speak with authority. All of this, paired with my stress and anxiety about different things, could easily send me into a panic. I realized this a couple of years ago, but did not comprehend it. I wanted to enjoy being around him, but his voice would trigger that same physical response and panic in me.

My sister-in-law has a very dominant personality and loud voice, and she is another trigger for me. I struggle in my relationship with her because her personality brings up anxiety and fear for me. I lock up and feel a distress that is at times suffocating, so I find there are times I have to stay away as a result.

When my daughters became toddlers, I started spanking them. I didn't know how else to discipline them. I knew I didn't want to hit them, but it took seeing their little eyes looking up at me, terrified, for me to recognize that I was in danger of scarring them the way I was scarred by physical abuse. I had a conversation with my husband and we agreed we were not going to spank our children anymore. Still, I didn't know how to get them to do what I wanted them to do in moments of frustration, so I began yelling at them instead. I felt it was a healthier alternative at the time, but still recognized the fear in their eyes and the disappointment in my husband's eyes when I was so mean to them. I knew these weren't healthy responses, but I didn't know how to stop. This is particularly vulnerable for me to share because it is with regards to my babies, but I am grateful to say that I am different now.

These oversized reactions were misplaced. Little things were causing disproportionate reactions in me. The same dynamic I experienced around conflict with my husband was evident in my discipline approach to my children.

I didn't know at first that these were all triggers for me—I thought my responses were just the way I was. Gradually, God started to reveal to me that these reactions were a response to my past, and that He could help me heal the trauma.

Once I realized that loud voices and aggressive personalities triggered me to react aggressively—and even violently—only then could I begin to make an effort to change. The process of healing slowly unraveled the tension I had been carrying inside for so many years. I no longer yell at my children. When they are having a fight or not listening—testing my patience—I stop and take a deep breath, and sometimes I need to tell myself, *Okay, calm down, it's not that big of a deal.* Once I have settled myself physically, I am able to think of an appropriate consequence in that moment. I have found taking privileges away for the day to be the most effective approach to addressing conflict and discipline. This is my go-to response now, and it really works. They listen and do what I need them to do much more often (not always—they are still children after all), and I feel better. There is no guilt and no fear of physical violence or aggression.

I became wired for violence and aggression. I know I have triggers and what kind of responses those triggers cause in me. I also know that those reactions are harmful to my family. So every time I feel I am getting ready to lose my temper, I remind myself that outbursts of anger are not from God, and I need to continue to make those desires obedient to God (Ephesians 4:31). I stop, take a deep breath, and think things through to come up with a healthy alternative to exploding in anger. I'm able to move beyond my triggers when they come up now. I know I am being triggered because I tense up, my chest hurts, and I can't breathe. With that awareness, I am called to take a moment to calm myself down before responding.

If there is one place our children need to feel completely safe, it should be in our homes. That is the kind of environment I want to raise my children in, because if they feel safe, they are more likely to tell me things—big and small—and to give me an opportunity to be there for them emotionally. Spanking and hitting children is very accepted in many cultures; however, no matter how you slice it, violence wires children for violence. Hitting was a default I learned in childhood. I needed to learn how to break that pattern.

Addressing my childhood trauma released the pent-up tension I was carrying around inside. There is so much more room in me now for patience, love, gentleness, and self-control. I am no longer hitting or yelling at my children and my husband, and it has had a beautiful effect on the atmosphere in my home. We are all more relaxed, and my kids are listening because taking away their privileges is much more effective than exploding and scaring everyone.

If you too struggle with this, and you know you are reacting in destructive ways under pressure, take it to God. He will show you the destructive ways in which you have been managing your pain and give you the strength to be different. If you lose control in specific situations, that's a trigger—you are acting out in ways you cannot control. If you wish you could respond differently but can't seem to, that's a button. You need to be aware of those moments and the feelings and reactions that they illicit so you can begin to take steps to change.

If you are unsure of what triggers you, ask God to show you the ways in which you are managing pain and fear and what the corresponding reactions are. Ask Him to show you, and He will. Remember, He wants to heal you, and He has led you to this point for a reason. We will do some of this together in Chapter 19.

BRINGING PAIN INTO VIEW

The journey of transforming my triggers and interior pain did not happen overnight. There was a whole season of my life in which I projected an exterior image of strength, but on the inside, I felt complete unworthy and incapable. I did a good job of hiding it. I spent a great deal of time on styling my hair and choosing outfits that projected professionalism. I had mastered an exterior of confidence, but the inside did not match the outside. I worked hard at projecting the person I wanted people to see, and it took me years to see that none if it matched how I felt. On the inside, I had angry talk on repeat, all the time. Realizing that I was really nasty in my thoughts was a pivotal moment.

It took a close relative calling me out on not being honest for me to see it. Someone close to my husband had a huge fallout with him because of it. She told him I was fake and phony and that she wanted nothing to do with me. It came as a shock to me. I thought to myself, "She is crazy—that's just not true. Does she want me to say out loud what I really think? I don't think she does! I don't think God does either!" I thought my effort made me blameless.

I was in denial, and that conflict forced me to take an honest look at myself. After about one year of this ongoing fight that had caused so much division in the family, I finally saw it for what it was and admitted it to myself. I was expending so much energy on smiling outwardly when I felt bitter on the inside. I was still so angry, and I thought I was doing people a favor by hiding it. I didn't know that people could see through me and that it was creating yet another barrier for me in my relationships. I was forcing smiles and kindness when on the inside I didn't trust anyone and had a rage that I knew I needed to tame, at least on the outside.

Today, I am working on mending that relationship because she helped me to realize that I had a lot of work to do inside me.

I know this is not something that is unique to me. This phenomenon is a result of unprocessed trauma and the anger we have hidden deep inside.

One of my closest friends and I were recently having an intimate conversation. My friend also has a history of trauma and abuse that began early in her life. She asked me with tears in her eyes, "When do I get to feel on the inside the way I am acting on the outside?" Hmm— the key word here is "acting." I knew exactly what she meant. We get used to performing to people's expectations. We give them the version of us we think they want. We mold ourselves to our circumstances and the people around us, never truly revealing who we really are, anywhere. As a result, we lose touch with who we are, and we need to remember. We need to confront our past, recognize who we became because of it, take responsibility for the actions we took as a result of it, and choose healing so that we can uncover who we truly are.

Ask God to reveal to you the areas that are being affected by your past abuse.

Desire – What do you want to know, heal, or change?
Depend – Is there something you read in this section about relying on God that you would like to bring forward with you?
Decide – What are you going to *do* differently in this area going forward?

Journal your thoughts.

What questions are coming up for you as you read?

Is there anything you are wrestling with God about?

Where do you see or feel you are being triggered? Take some time to think about this over the next few days.

Is there an area of your life where you are really struggling in relationships?

Do certain people cause you to immediately feel tense, angry or anxious?

What could be causing that?

What are your buttons?

CHAPTER 14

Choice, Free Will and Obedience

Y ou have probably heard it said that we are in control of nothing because God is in control of everything. That is true, but He has also given us a free will and authority over our life in the choices that we make.

What is the impact of the choices we make?

BREAKING THE CYCLE

We all make choices, every second of every day. These choices are powerful. They shape the environment of our minds, our hearts, and our homes. The power of choice is about breaking generational issues. The Bible is clear on the severity of worshiping anything other than the one true God. The Bible calls these *idols*. An idol can be anything that takes a place of importance above God in your heart. It can be our careers, an ambition for material or financial success, or it could even be a relationship in our lives. The Bible tells us that the consequence of worshiping idols affects our future generations. Even the children of children are affected when people choose to ignore and disobey God—up to the third and fourth generation. I believe this is why my family has lived in the darkness of abuse for generations. Someone needed to choose differently to turn the tide and bring in the protective love of God. It also tells us He favors a thousand generations for those who love and follow His commands. You can find this right at the beginning of the Ten Commandments. That shows you how important that commandment is to God and to us (Exodus 20:4-6). One-thousand generations ahead of you are depending on the choices you make today. No pressure!

As parents, we are blessed with the great responsibility of protecting and guiding the children God has placed in our care. We can be very intentional about the environment we create for ourselves and our children. Our choices have the power to create an atmosphere of safety and love for our children, or they can leave our children vulnerable to countless risks. Whatever we decide to let into our lives by way of relationships, experiences, exposure and entertainment, our children inevitably come along for the ride.

The environment my parents created for us left us vulnerable. My mother, being the sole-provider at the time, had no choice but to leave me in the care of others, at times alone with my father who was rarely sober. My father was addicted to alcohol, and his dependence on it and other drugs clouded his judgement and his ability to be present for me. Today I am well aware that environments where alcohol is the center of the party usually end in family fights, language that is inappropriate for little ears, and a lot of distraction. I chose to raise my daughters differently. My husband doesn't drink. I enjoy a glass of wine occasionally, but we rarely visit or entertain with alcohol. We are cautious of what we watch and listen to. We want to protect them from receiving skewed messages about life. We talk to our children regularly about life, struggles, and events that happen because we don't want to shelter them to the point where they are unaware and unprepared for life later. We have made these conscious choices to protect them and ourselves.

You are powerful and influential in your family. Your children are watching, listening, and learning from you and the environment they are growing up in, whether you realize it or not. Even before they seem to grasp what is happening around them, they will remember, and when they are older things will come into focus for them. I urge you to be careful what you allow in your home in terms of entertainment, people, and consumption of alcohol and other drugs that you know are harmful for you and distract you from being your best around your children and family.

WHERE WAS GOD? A DISCUSSION ABOUT FREE WILL

What happened to me was not because He allowed it or because He watched idly by as the innocence of His creation was destroyed. What happened to me was a result of free will.

I spent many years asking, "Where was God?" That unanswered question drove me to give myself permission to act out in anger and defense. When little girls are taught in their fragile years that love and affection are attached to touching in ways that make them uncomfortable, they are programmed to go through life allowing trespass after trespass. As a child, I learned that grownups are the authority. I was not to question or disobey them. I was told to listen to them. This resulted in blind obedience. When grownups we love and trust have full access to us, we are powerless and stand quietly by as the peace and beauty of life is snatched from us.

What happened to you was a result of someone else's free will. Someone made some evil choices around you. If you were swept away as a result of someone else's free will, you can place responsibility for what happened to you on the person who made those evil choices and not on God.

I'm going to bring this up again here because I think it's very important. I've had many conversations with friends where people have turned away from God as a result of being hurt by *people*. You may have been let down by the Church. You may struggle with the encouragement throughout this book to trust God. If your abuse happened in a church or was perpetrated by a spiritual leader, I'm so sorry that happened—and this abuse particularly grieves the heart of our Father—but please don't blame God. People can be awful representatives of God and not all who claim to be Christian are truly seeking to follow in the footsteps of Jesus. As human beings, we are sinful, broken, and selfish people. We are going to continue to disappoint one another.

You have the power to make choices to ensure that that cycle of violence and trauma stops here and your children have a different story to tell going forward.

CHOOSING OBEDIENCE

"Okay God, I'm here. You have my attention."

Deciding you are going to walk in obedience is hard. There are things I've had to let go of, things I really enjoyed but knew weren't good for me. I used to do many of the things people fear the Church will tell them not to do. I stopped doing them not because anyone at church said so, but because I knew they were not good for me. For example, I stopped watching sexually explicit content on Netflix. I even stopped listening to some of my very favorite boss lady singers because of the sexually explicit nature of the lyrics. I struggled for a while with whether or not I should stop drinking. The Bible doesn't outright call it a sin, it says, "Don't be drunk with wine, because that will ruin your life" (Ephesians 5:8, NLT). I have seen what alcohol does to families. My childhood is a prime example of what happens in a home lacking direction from God and centered on alcoholism. More on that later. I also decided to remove my piercings—the ones no one could see except my husband and God. I've had to make choices to avoid big and small things that seem inconsequential.

Beyond giving up things that are not good for us, what does walking in obedience really mean? When I decided to turn to God for guidance in all things, I didn't anticipate He would ask me to do some things I really didn't feel like doing. I learned that obedience means that *I don't do the things I know are not good for me* even if it's hard, and that *I do things that are good for me,* whether I feel like it or not!

Deciding you are going to walk in obedience can be scary. I hesitated for a time, knowing that there might be things in my life that didn't please God and that I may be called to change or leave them. I believe many of us shy away from pursuing a relationship with God precisely because we fear having to change.

And this is true—you may need to change; but change is not something God expects will happen overnight, or *by your own strength*. As you lean further into Him, He will begin to reveal to you the things that do not help you but, rather, seek to destroy you. He will reveal them and give you the strength to abstain from them. It will be hard for a time, but eventually the strength of your desires for those things will decrease and your ability to walk in obedience will grow. And another thing: The things that are harmful for you may not all be the same as those I struggle with. In each situation, we must examine our heart, our motives, and priorities. Once you are aware that something is disrupting your peace, creating conflict in your marriage, creating problems in your relationships, or placing you in situations that could be otherwise harmful, you may decide you do not want to engage in those things any more. By His strength, you will gain the willpower to not only identify but overcome those temptations and desires. As you grow in your *faith*, you will also grow in *obedience*.

If you're having trouble with the idea of obedience, perhaps you are thinking about it in a different way than God intends. Obedience is not about staying within a list of rules; it's rather about strengthening us and helping us to live the joy-filled life we have been promised.

When I prayed for guidance in every aspect of my life, I began to sense as a whisper in my mind that said, "Imagine what your life would look like if you decided to walk in obedience." I wasn't sure what that meant initially, but sure enough, God began to slowly reveal to me the things that didn't fill me with joy but instead robbed me of it, and I gradually felt naturally inclined to give those things up. I no longer desire or enjoy sexually explicit content in shows, movies, or music. I know those visuals only stir within me lust and tempt me to think of those images when I really want to walk in purity. Same sex activity between women is common on television. I know what that stirs in me—a temptation of my past sins—so I avoid that type of content. I removed my body jewelry, not because I believe that it is inherently bad or sinful; I chose to remove them because I seek to please God and regardless of how insignificant, superficial, and small this gesture is, I know that what God notices and focuses on is my desire to please Him in even the smallest things. When I was still living in a lot of emotional turmoil, I had made a habit of drinking wine pretty regularly. It was a habit that grew over time, to the point that I needed to have a glass or two every night and would stop at the grocery story every couple of days to ensure I never ran out. I used it to soothe my anxieties, to help me relax, and calm myself into sleep. As you can see, it wasn't a healthy occasional treat but rather a way of numbing and soothing when I really should have been going to God for the peace I wanted.

I struggled with this for a time. I was feeling guilty over having even a small amount of wine even when I was not drinking excessively. I had heard conflicting opinions from Christians on this issue, and I wanted to resolve and settle what was God's will for this issue in my life. On one hand, I had read scriptures that tell us Jesus' first miracle in his ministry was when he turned water into wine (John 2). The Bible repeatedly mentions wine as a good thing but warns about not drinking to drunkenness. Then there is 1 Timothy 5:23 (NLV), "You ought to drink a little wine." I joked about this scripture once with some girlfriends when I came across it, saying I was going to make T-shirts and how I really liked Timothy.

There are two perspectives on this, those who don't see it as a sin because of what I've already mentioned (I tend to side with that camp) and those who say, "You are not a true Christian if you drink alcohol." Someone literally said that to me not long ago. So I needed to reconcile that too.

I decided to take this to God, look at the scriptures, and sought advice from my wise Christian friends. I wondered if my struggle was related to the history of alcoholism in my family. I realized I had adopted a negative association with alcohol and viewed it as a destructive thing based on the abuses I had seen and how their addictions gripped people in my family.

I knew then that this was something the enemy was using to accuse me of not being in right standing with God. I also recognized that I had potential to consume alcohol to unhealthy levels in the past and for the wrong reasons. In the end, I decided that I would enjoy some wine occasionally because if Jesus, who was perfect and sinless, made wine miraculously, then it wasn't inherently bad or sinful for me. I want to be really careful that you do not perceive this as a blanket statement of alcohol being a good or bad thing. You will need to evaluate for yourself what is good or harmful to your life and spiritual walk. That goes for all things, not just the examples of the things I have struggled with and share here.

SEEK HIS WILL FOR YOUR LIFE

If you are thinking of something in your life that may or may not need to be brought into obedience to God and removed from your life, here is some practical guidance to test your choices. I use this formula in my decision making faithfully, and it always yields the best outcome for me. The answer isn't always the one I want, but that's where choosing obedience is crucial.

Give God the first and final word on whatever it is you are contemplating to change.

Seek his will in all you do, and he will show you which path to take.
— Proverbs 3:6 (NLT)

1. What does the Bible say on the subject? You can quickly search your Bible app for a keyword and review scriptures that reference the topic.

And so, my children, listen to me for all
who follow my ways are joyful.
— Proverbs 9: 32 (NLT)

2. Seek advice from the wise people in your life.

*For lack of guidance a nation falls, but victory
is won through many advisers.*
– Proverbs 11:14 (NIV)

3. Always give God the final say. Ask Him in prayer to search your heart and, if there is anything in you that does not please Him, ask Him to help you to change and walk in obedience (Psalm 139:23-24).

4. Try it on for size. Take your two choices and journal how you see things going if you choose that thing. Ask yourself these questions: *If I go this route, what would happen? How would I feel? How would it affect my loved ones?* Follow it through as far as your imagination will take you. Do this exercise with both of your options. Imagine that you have made up your mind for option A, sit with that choice for a few days, and see how it feels inside of you. After two or three days of placing yourself in that decision (without taking any action yet—this is an exercise in discerning the will of God), do the same for option B.

5. Evaluate: How do each of these choices feel on the inside? What do you sense God is saying to you in this area? You may know by now which is the wiser choice.

Be still in the presence of the Lord, and wait patiently for him to act.
– Psalm 37:7

I do this when I am facing major decisions but also small ones when I am unsure of how to proceed. I desire to please God and to listen to His guidance.

I do this even in the little things, like when I desire a glass of wine. I kid you not, I have been at the market plenty of times contemplating, "God, should I buy a bottle of wine or not?" I have to honestly reflect, *Am I desiring it just because I want to enjoy it with a special meal I am making, or among friends, or am I trying to escape some feeling or situation?* Many times, I have left the aisle empty handed, and yet others I have walked away with a bottle of red wine and enjoyed it without experiencing any residual guilt after having it. That is what pleases God, a heart that desires to please Him, seeks Him in the big and the small, and invites Him into every area of your life.

CHOICE AND HEALING

As you go through this process of healing, you are going to have to make choices, and some of them are going to be bold and scary. The key is to trust that God is going to be there for you, that He's going to guide you as you take those steps, and catch you when you leap forward. He is here for you, but you are going to have to choose to move forward. That choice is always yours. The ball is in your court.

He has given us free will, and He respects our authority over our lives, so we have to choose to take steps in His direction in order for Him to flourish in our lives.

> *But if serving the Lord seems undesirable to you, then choose for yourselves this day whom you will serve, whether the gods your ancestors served beyond the Euphrates, or the gods of the Amorites, in whose land you are living. But as for me and my household, we will serve the Lord.*
> *– Joshua 24:15 (NIV)*

When I embarked on this work myself, I had many fears and doubts, among them: *Am I really going to be able to do this? Am I ready? Am I educated enough? Am I healed enough?* And yet, it was when I stepped into this work that my confidence grew and my ability to express my experience was ignited. It was then that healing ultimately took hold in my life.

Once I made the choice to move forward into my healing, I felt connected to God in a way I had never experienced before. When I was an adolescent and sought Him, I felt His presence, but my healing season in particular was, and still is, a season of growth and power in my life like I have never experienced before. This is a next-level relationship with God—an intimacy I had only heard of in worship songs, one that I desired but didn't fully understand.

SURRENDER YOUR WILL

Daily Choices
What do you feed your heart and your mind with (music, TV, conversations)?

The Believer's Freedom
"I have the right to do anything," you say—
but not everything is beneficial.
"I have the right to do anything"—but not everything is constructive.
– 1 Corinthians 10:23 (NIV)

Your choices matter. Everything from the people you bring around your family, the music you listen to, the television you watch, and other forms of entertainment you may consume have a direct impact on your life and the lives of those around you.

I have become aware of the influence that music and entertainment can have on my life. As a result, I am very careful about what I feed my mind. Certain visuals on television also stayed with me, causing me to feel fearful or angry, or they stirred in me an attraction toward women, a dangerous thought to allow to grow within me, if I want to protect my marriage, family, and soul.

These small choices can have big impacts on our lives.

Abstaining from sexual lyrical and visual content helped to silence the intruding thoughts I had struggled with for decades and, ultimately, resulted in a growth in desire for my husband.

As a mother of two young children, I was often busy around the clock and was usually wiped out by the time I would leave my girls sleeping in their rooms. That's when I used to turn to the TV to disconnect, unplug my mind from the busyness of my life, and consume the latest show on Netflix. Much of what I found contained heavy and explicit sexual scenes.

Consuming graphic content stirred my sexual desires. At times, I wanted to sleep with my husband not because I desired closeness with him but simply because I wanted to satisfy the urges created from what I was watching on television. Most of the time, however, I was too tired and uninterested in intimacy with my husband, so I turned to satisfying my desires alone and in secret. I got into a damaging cycle of satisfying myself and quieting my urges without my husband.

I didn't know it then, but I see now that I was robbing him of that which belonged to him. Once I realized this, I decided to stop watching sexually explicit shows and had less desire to satisfy my urges alone. Ultimately, my desire for my husband grew, and I began to enjoy him more intimately between the sheets.

God calls us to purity for our own good. Intimacy with my husband has grown in and out of the bedroom because of the healing and transformation that He brought about in my soul.

There are a lot of distractions out there. The sexually explicit nature of the lyrics in many songs also caused my mind to wander. It wasn't only the sexually explicit content either; there were romantic songs that stirred in me a longing for the past. They reminded me of past relationships in what they were saying and transported me into a fantasy world in which people in my past looked so perfect from a distance. I could no longer see all of the reasons why the relationship didn't happen or why it ended, but instead would flash back to only the first few days in which things were exciting and new.

Over time, it became such that I was comparing my life with my husband to the fantasy world in my mind. I had built up perfect fantasies in my mind of what a relationship with a man should look and feel like, and I became ungrateful for the imperfect but committed and loving man I had for real—the one who could hug me, love me, and had made a promise before God to be with only me.

I am not saying that all music is inherently bad, but could it be that certain types of music are causing you to live dissatisfied and blind to the blessing you have by your side? That was so for me for a time. And, given my family's history with infidelity-as you read, my mother's unhealed trauma led her to bitterness and cheating-I am adamant about protecting my own family.

What do we have to lose, after all, in giving ourselves to God? Perhaps a few friends, some forms of entertainment, the crutches we lean on emotionally to get through life such as food, sugar, certain types of music and other addictions. Honestly, when I look at it in my own life, I realize that what I will lose are things that don't help me in my life anyway. Yet what I have to gain is a healthy, joy-filled life, the beautiful future that He promises us both on this earth and eternally.

What good is it for someone to gain the
whole world, yet forfeit their soul?
– Mark 8:36 (NIV)

—————————— Contemplation ——————————

In your journal, write the answers to the following questions underneath the words *Desire, Depend,* and *Decide.*

Desire – What do you want to know, heal, or change?
Depend – Is there something you read in this section about relying on God that you would like to bring forward with you?
Decide – What are you going to *do* differently in this area going forward?

Journal your thoughts.

What questions are coming up for you as you read?

Is there anything you are wrestling with God about?

CHAPTER 15

Unbraiding

SHAME AND REPENTANCE

There might be choices you have made that have caused you to feel guilt or remorse; part of your healing is to acknowledge the things you chose that were not good for you or others. I arrived at a point in my healing in which I felt convicted for some of the things I did after I was abused. As I shared before, after I was abused, I began playing physical games with another child that involved touching. For many years, I rationalized and silenced my guilt by saying to myself that the odd games I played were a result of the odd games that were played with me. I see now that I was acting out in sinful ways by choice. Regardless of where I learned these behaviors, instinctively I knew they were wrong, and that's why I did them in secret. I already carried shame for what had been done to me by the people who abused me, and my actions only added to that shame. I had made a choice and had done something harmful to someone else.

The age in which I gave my body away to men caused me to be further tangled in shame. Early in my adult life, I also let some men go further intimately with me than I was comfortable. I can see now that I gave my body when I was pressured because I thought my heart and body were a package deal. The abuse I experienced taught me that love and affection come with touching and the taking of my body. I lost my power to say, "NO, STOP, I am not comfortable with that, and I will not do what you want." The powerlessness I had experienced in silence at a young age led me to make those allowances later, which only increased my shame.

Those hurtful choices (to myself and others) were what grew from what happened to me. Later in life, I had the freedom to choose what I would do with my own life.

I needed to see all of that for what it was, and to acknowledge that I was carrying around a burden that didn't belong to me. The shame I was handed by the people who abused me needed to be seen and released from my life. The lies I lived by needed truth to expose them.

Next, I needed to own *my* choices and actions and deal with the guilt I rightfully felt for the bad things I had done as a result of the abuse I experienced. Recall that I didn't learn appropriate sexual boundaries as a child, and my ability to discern right from wrong was compromised at a young age because the people who I looked up to for guidance, instruction, and protection were doing evil things around me and to me. As a result, the good and the bad became one tangled, confusing mess, and I needed to sort through that mess and ***unbraid it.***

The Merriam-Webster Dictionary defines a ***braid*** as three or more interweaving strands,[8] and ***unbraiding*** as separating or unraveling them.[9] I unraveled in the season of my healing in the best of ways.

To unbraid means to release the shame we feel for the sins committed against us by our abusers and from the guilt we feel for the choices we made of our own free will as a result.

There was a time when I thought, "I am this way because of what happened to me. I'm just mean, inflexible, and angry. I was built that way. Period." I needed to begin to take responsibility for myself in order to be set free from the things that were holding me down. The abuse I experienced led to promiscuity, and, early in adulthood, I had an

---

[8] https://www.merriam-webster.com/dictionary/braid
[9] https://www.merriam-webster.com/dictionary/unbraid

incorrect perspective of relationships with men. I learned that emotional and physical attention were tied to one another. That lie drove a lot of my actions back then. I allowed men to go further with me sexually than I was comfortable as a result. I needed to take responsibility for those choices and actions. I could have easily continued to say, "I was abused sexually, and that's why I am the way I am, and that's why I did the things I did"—but that's not taking responsibility for my own actions. Yes, I was molested; yes, I was entangled in the shame of my abuse and anger because I was not protected by the adults responsible for me; and yes, I felt guilt over the choices I made. I learned wrongful ideas of what it means to be in relationships with men, but I, of my own free will, made those allowances with the men in my life once I was an adult. I needed to own that, confess it to God, ask Him to forgive me, and choose to change.

Perhaps you, too, feel ashamed about the good feelings that are tangled up with the bad ones. I want to reassure you here that just because you have some good memories and feelings about your abuser doesn't place any responsibility on you for the abuse. Again, you were a child. You were unable to discern the strategies at play in the games that were played with you. You did not have sufficient knowledge, maturity, or authority to consent to such a relationship. Your abuser took advantage of your innocence and trust.

As children, we loved and desired affection, possibly even from our abusers, and because of that we can feel ashamed and responsible for what happened. We need to release the responsibility that we wrongfully assumed through our abuse.

I loved my uncle and wanted his attention, but it came with the bad stuff. Being a child and not knowing the implications of the touching created so much confusion in me. I grew up in that confusion and needed to reach a point where I understood it so I could *unbraid it*, or separate it in order to release the shame I carried for what had been done to me.

Also, you may have enjoyed the love, affection, and attention you received during a time when you were vulnerable. Your desire for love was given to you by God for the purpose of bonding with your parents and caregivers. You were designed to crave and desire love and affection. The fact that that love was given to you along with evil does not make any of it your fault. You were, and are, not responsible for that.

At any age, we need touch and affection, but when it is delivered in such an evil way by people we love and trust, it creates shame in us because of our God-given desire and need for it. The good becomes so entangled with the bad that it becomes really difficult to understand what's what. There is a separation that needs to happen within us, where we recognize and separate the sins of others from our being.

I call this process "unbraiding it."

Here's an explanation of the braid metaphor that will help you heal from your childhood trauma.

Imagine a braid that contains three separate strands. Braided together, they become one composite piece, making it difficult to distinguish what belongs to which strand. Within the braid, we have three components: shame, anger, and guilt. Shame is what gets planted deep inside us when we experience abuse at the hands of people. Anger is the scar tissue left by our childhood wounds; like a screen through which we view life, it influences us as we interact with others after we have been profoundly wounded. Guilt is the feeling within us that tells us we have done something harmful to ourselves or others. God is the only one who can release you from the shame of your abuse, heal your anger, and free you from a guilty conscience; thus, He is the One who drives the process of separating the three strands of the braid. When you reach for God, He is the force that pulls apart the intertwined or entangled shame, anger, and guilt.

REPENTING

Guilt is a gift from God that tells us we have done something wrong. That guilt is what leads us to repentance—the desire to change and to do things differently going forward. Guilt is a gift from God—it is meant to guide us back into right standing with Him. This feeling drives us to admit that we have made a mistake. It is meant to lead us to say, "I'm sorry," and repent (change our ways). Were there decisions you made later on in life that stemmed from the abuse you experienced? Is there something in your past that you feel guilty about? If you are feeling guilty for something you have done, lean into that feeling. Let it guide you into confession and repentance. In the Bible, God urges us to confess our sins to Him for forgiveness. Speaking our secrets out loud to God, and to others with words, and asking for forgiveness is how we are cleansed.

Each of you must repent of your sins and turn to God, and be baptized in the name of Jesus Christ for the forgiveness of your sins. Then you will receive the gift of the Holy Spirit.
– Acts 2:38

God gave us *confession* as a means to set us free from **shame** (inherited by us through the sins committed against us) and **guilt** (for the sinful choices we ourselves have made). When we give words to our struggles, the ghosts that haunt us in the secret places of our mind can no longer torment us. Light eliminates darkness. Let it shine; talk to God. Only He can set you free.

Remember that *prayer* is how you can communicate with God. He is all-knowing and ever-present. If you feel compelled to do so, you may also confess your struggles out loud to a trusted friend who you know will not judge you but instead will pray for you to help you heal. We were left this instruction in the Bible so you know you can trust it.

Confess your sins to each other and pray for each other so that you may be healed.
The earnest prayer of a righteous person has great power and produces wonderful results.
– James 5:16 (NLT)

Don't misunderstand me; I don't believe that God requires a public confession. I have been inspired to share my experience with the world for the sake of others so that God can be glorified. I've said it before; I want you to know what happened to me, what I have done, and what He has done for me; and who I am today. Because if He forgave, cleansed, and healed me, He will certainly do the same for you if you ask Him to. God is the only one who can forgive us and set us free from our guilt.

You have a direct line to Him: The only intermediary you need is Jesus. He came to earth as a sacrifice for our sins and as a bridge between you and God. Pray all things in the name of Jesus, and God will hear and answer your prayers according to His highest will.

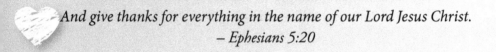

And give thanks for everything in the name of our Lord Jesus Christ.
– Ephesians 5:20

Talk to Him—He is with you right now, and He has been waiting for you to speak to Him all this time.

Recall that after I was molested, I began playing boyfriend and girlfriend games with two children close to my age. These games involved sexual touching. For most of my life, I lived with the shame of what happened to me and the guilt of what I had done. For years, I rationalized that those games were just innocent games among children. Eventually, I realized that they were inappropriate and harmful, the result of the abusive games that had been played with me.

As an adult, I came to understand that what happened to me between the ages of five and ten years old was not my fault. However, it was difficult to release the guilt I felt for the games I had initiated and played later of my own free will. I was a child in an awful situation, learning very bad things from the people who hurt me, and I mimicked their behavior in the games I played later. I learned a distorted concept of affection. That distorted perspective led to some bad behavior when I was a child and later in my adult life when I played touching games with other girls, gave my body to men who didn't deserve it, and eventually experimented with women, questioning my sexuality. I know now that my body isn't mine to give freely in the first place—we are called to live in purity.

Treat older women as you would your mother, and treat younger women with all purity as you would your own sisters.
– 1 Timothy 5:2 (NLT)

When I first opened up this conversation with God, it was because I began to feel a heaviness in my heart and felt stirred to reach out to a friend. I told him I needed to confess some things and needed prayer. I told him of the games of sexual touching I played as a child, and we prayed for God to forgive me and to deliver me of the shame.

For years, I felt deeply ashamed of what I had done. I also reached out to one of the girls I had inappropriately touched when we were kids and said I was sorry for the inappropriate games and for touching her. I told her about the abuse I experienced, and I asked her to forgive me. She said she forgave me and that I should not feel bad about it.

The second child I had played inappropriately with was slightly younger than me, which also caused me a lot of shame my whole life. I have no way of reaching her, and I have no idea her whereabouts. I don't even know her last name. I wish I could reach her because it pains me to think that I introduced evil into her life and that out there somewhere there may be a woman living with the consequences of my actions. To her I say, from the bottom of my heart, "I'm sorry. I'm sorry for what I did to you. I'm sorry that I played those inappropriate games when we were just children. I'm sorry for what that may have caused in your life. Perhaps that led you to do things later that you are now ashamed of. I'm sorry for introducing the darkness that had attached to me into your life. I pray that God will enlighten you and release you from that as well."

When I first thought about that season in my preteen years, it was easier to think that those games were simply a result of the confusion created within me by those who abused me; but God clarified this for me later. I realized that I, too, had made choices even at that young of an age. I chose to follow my sexual desires and sinned. I sinned against those girls, against my body, and most importantly, against God. And those sins were haunting me all these years later. I was already married with children and yet still strangely and secretly attracted to women and fighting off the memories of things I had done. I needed to recognize this, acknowledge it, and take responsibility for it. Only then could God forgive me, release me from the shame that bound me, and heal me from it.

If you are reading this and you are similarly coming into an awareness of actions you took in your life that may have been tied to your abuse and are weighed down by a sense of guilt, I encourage you to ask God for forgiveness. If you feel stirred to apologize to someone in your life directly, do so. Perhaps the person or people you hurt are not accessible to you, or you are simply not ready to have a conversation. Know that you can still be forgiven. If you are feeling guilty (convicted) for something you did in your past, bow your head right now and ask God to forgive you for what you did. Choose to speak with God—He will deliver you. In fact, He already has. He sent His one and only Son to earth with you in mind, so that you could have someone to reach for. He already carried and took all your burdens to the cross . . . you just didn't know it, and so you continued to carry the secrets. Over time, even holding up our empty hands can become unbearably heavy. You can put the burden down now. Leave it behind and move forward into the life He promised you.

Once I released this guilt to God in my own life, the most amazing thing happened: The negative thoughts lost their power over me. They would still pop up in certain moments with my children, but I knew that the thoughts were not urges, tendencies, or the desires of my heart, but rather were the result of something that had attached to my mind during my abuse. Bringing that darkness into the light with my words and my confession made it so the thoughts no longer had power over me.

TRANSFORMING YOUR MINDSET ─────────────

Throughout my life, when I chose to lash out in my anger at the people around me—my family, acquaintances, and even strangers—those were also choices I made. I allowed the memories of my painful experiences to rise out of my subconscious into the present and lingered in them, allowing them to affect how I behaved toward others. When I was growing up, I felt justified in behaving this way toward my mother, stepfather, and brother when I felt mistreated, but later this pattern became my default, and it controlled me instead of the other way around. Anger and defensiveness became automatic responses from me toward the world, and people around me, to the point that I didn't pause to think before reacting; it was simply habit.

> *"Everything we do is first a thought we build into our brains. The root of everything you say and do is based on the memories you have built into your brain through your thinking. Memories take time to build (twenty-one days to build a long-term memory and another forty-two days to build this memory into a thinking habit).*[10]

If you are interested in learning more about how our memories can be transformed into new thinking habits, I highly recommend you read Dr. Leaf's book, *Think, Learn, Succeed,* for further study on the mind-brain connection.

Be careful of the thoughts you allow to take space inside of you because they can grow to take over your life. Our experiences get recorded in our brain physically. Dr. Leaf asserts that memories take up physical real estate in the brain[11] and that what we entertain in our thoughts grows physically in our brain establishing thought patterns that we later operate out of automatically. This is exactly what happened to me. I was treating others unfairly, living out of a victim

[10] Leaf, Dr. Caroline. *Think, Learn, Succeed: Understanding and Using Your Mind to Thrive at School, the Workplace, and Life.* Baker Books, 2019.
[11] Leaf, Dr. Caroline. *Think, Learn, Succeed. Ibid.*

state, hyperaware, hypersensitive, and explosive to those closest to me because I wanted to protect myself from further harm. This was unfair to people who came into my life later and had nothing to do with my past experiences. I needed to acknowledge and repent of this and choose to behave differently going forward so that my memory system could be healed over time.

Contemplation

In your journal, write the answers to the following questions underneath the words *Desire, Depend,* and *Decide.*

Desire – What do you want to know, heal, or change?
Depend – Is there something you read in this section about relying on God that you would like to bring forward with you?
Decide – What are you going to *do* differently in this area going forward?

Journal your thoughts.

What questions are coming up for you as you read?

Is there anything you are wrestling with God about?

CHAPTER 16

What Does It Mean to be Healed?

A NEW CREATION

God promised He would make you new.

Do not remember the former things, nor consider the things of old.
Behold, I will do a new thing, now it shall spring forth;
Shall you know it?
I will even make a road in the wilderness and rivers in the desert.
— Isaiah 43:18-19

HOW DO YOU GET THERE?

God forgives the repented heart, heals them, and gives them peace.
— Isaiah 57:19

When we are children and developing, we are fertile ground for creating the foundation on which our life will stand. As a child, you were rich and ready soil for the planting of the tree you would become over time. Then life—your surroundings, your family, and circumstances—began to sprinkle seeds atop that soil. The seeds that were sown into you eventually sprouted and grew into who you became.

Parable of the Farmer Scattering Seed
"Listen! A farmer went out to plant some seed. As he scattered it across his field, some of the seed fell on a footpath, and the birds came and ate it. Other seed fell on shallow soil with underlying rock. The seed sprouted quickly because the soil was shallow. But the plant soon wilted under the hot sun, and since it didn't have deep roots, it died. Other seed fell among thorns that grew up and choked out the tender plants so they produced no grain. Still other seeds fell on fertile soil, and they sprouted, grew, and produced a crop that was thirty, sixty, and even a hundred times as much as had been planted!"
—Mark 4:3-8 (NLT)

When violence, abuse, and pain are sown, what will grow out of them? The abuse you experienced were the seeds from which many weeds grew. The attitudes and behaviors that resulted later were the fruits that came from those seeds.

A beautiful tree was in the midst of the thickness of those weeds; it was hard to see and a bit malnourished of the sunlight it needed. But the light from above, God, is so persistent, so faithful, so loving that He reached me through the brush. God has transformed me into something new. He planted new seeds, and all around me there is new life. He sowed into my soil forgiveness, love, patience, comfort, and kindness, and today I am bearing those fruits.

I will always have scars from my past, but I am healed. The garden that has sprouted in my life is blooming beauty and love all around me.

As long as I continue to water the garden, it will continue to grow in strength and power.

Abuse took much from me. I can see now that it also gifted me some beautiful things. Those early life experiences shaped me into the woman I am today: resilient, compassionate, trustworthy, a fierce protector of children, and determined to help women break free from the effects of abuse that persist in their subconscious minds. The greatest gift I received was my faith in God. Leaning on my Creator has been my refuge. He sustained me through the darkest of times and didn't give up on me, even during my rebellious years. You may recall, there was a time when I blamed Him for all that had happened, and wanted nothing to do with Him. He stood at my side, patiently loving me and waiting—waiting for the day I would return to Him and ask Him to reveal Himself to me and heal me.

There is a story in the Bible about a woman who suffered for twelve years of a bleeding disorder. She had used all of her resources going to doctors, but her condition only worsened. Unable to find help or healing, she reached for Jesus among a large crowd and was healed by faith alone. With full confidence, she thought to herself, ***If I can just touch his robe, I will be healed*** (Mark 5:28, NLT). "Immediately her bleeding stopped and she knew she had been healed of her terrible condition" (Mark 5:29, NLT). Any one of us can be like that woman. The moment she touched the hem of His clothes, Jesus felt power leave Him. He asked His disciples, "Who touched me?" The woman responded, saying it had been her.

And he said to her, "Daughter, your faith has made
you well. Go in peace. Your suffering is over."
— Mark 5:34 (NLT)

After I left my career in government, God guided me along a path of healing. There were seven specific moments that He used to unlock my heart. Those "7 Steps Toward Healing" changed my life. In the next chapter, I will share those moments with you. I hope they inspire you and give you some tools to reach for God and the life He promised you in the Bible. You may not fully understand how right now, but with His help, you, too, can step into healing and ensure that the cycle of abuse ends with you. As you read about these seven healing moments, I encourage you to examine your own heart and life and reach for God in prayer as I did. He guided you to this book because He wants to heal you. If you *desire* to be healed, *depend* on Him, and *decide* to reach for Him, your life will never be the same again.

The 7 Steps Toward Healing are conversation starters for you to talk to God. This framework will guide you through a series of reflections and conversations, and will invite you to reach for God in prayer. This process is best done in partnership with a trusted friend, spouse, mentor, pastor, or other person you feel safe with. As you will read, a few close friends, my husband, and my in-laws were instrumental in my healing journey. Through them I received validation, support, and comfort. If you do not have someone you feel safe confiding in, you can choose to do the steps on your own with a journal as your partner. The key to healing is honesty with God and with yourself.

God will meet you right where you are and deliver healing where you need it with the people you have around you. Healing is not one-size-fits-all. This framework is a guide. You may already be walking through your own healing process and not even know it. You may discover you have already started working through some of the steps in this framework. Also, healing is not a linear process, and you may have experienced some of these but not in the same order. Perhaps you are in the middle of this process and don't recognize it now. Within each of the steps, I will share how they unfolded in my life and give you some guidance to work these steps in your own healing. Healing is as unique as you are. This framework, however, will give you a path to follow in the company of God. It is not necessary for you to spend time trying to figure out what has or has not already been healed in you. He knows. He sees you through and through, and He will deliver what you need exactly when you need it.

Confession, prayer, repentance, and forgiveness are at the foundation of this process—God's process for your healing. I don't call it my process because it isn't mine—it's His. He walked me through it; He connected the dots for me to see how each of them fit together and led me to new levels and areas that needed to be healed. I documented these steps in a framework that can be applied by others because if He did it for me, I know He will do it again and again for any of His children who choose to seek Him—the Bible tells us so. The following scriptures are provided for you to see that this is the Will of God for your life, to heal you:

Biblical Foundation of 7 Steps Toward Healing

Confession

If we confess our sins,
he is faithful and just and will forgive us our sins and
purify us from all unrighteousness.
— 1 John 1:9 (NIV)

Confession and Prayer

Therefore, confess your sins to each other and
pray for each other so that you may be healed.
The prayer of a righteous person is powerful and effective.
— James 5:16 (NIV)

Repentance

Whoever conceals their sins does not prosper, but
the one who confesses and renounces them finds mercy.
— Proverbs 28:13 (NIV)

Forgiveness

Finally, I confessed all my sins to you
and stopped trying to hide my guilt.
I said to myself, "I will confess my rebellion to the Lord."
And you forgave me! All my guilt is gone.
— Psalm 32:5

DOING OUR PART WHILE FOLLOWING
GUIDANCE FROM GOD ————————————————

It's so easy for us to rely on ourselves and feel completely alone in our efforts to heal and succeed in life. I constantly have to remind myself that, ultimately, God is in control and He is working things in my favor, even when I can't see everything fits together or their purpose—particularly when things are hard. It's true: Ultimately, God is in control, and He designed this life to work perfectly. That said, the world gets in the way at times and we take detours. God has gifted us with abilities to help us in all areas of our lives and we should not just sit back and wait for God to deliver a miracle, but rather, we can take steps in faith, moving in the direction of what we hope for. We can do our best with what He has given to us, trusting that He who sees all the parts involved in the past, present, and future, has our best interest in mind. Let that be the faith that moves you forward and watch that faith in action materialize into the desires of your heart.

"I know the plans I have for you," declares the Lord,
"plans to prosper you and not to harm you,
plans to give you hope and a future."
— Jeremiah 29:11

I don't want to rely on myself, but I also know when God is calling me to take steps. We cannot sit on the couch and wait for God to deliver a blessing. He has equipped us, and we need to make a choice and take some actions in faith. He will provide wisdom and bring the right resources and people, He will open doors and provide inspiration, but we certainly have a role to play in our own healing and in the outcome of our lives.

FORGIVENESS ─────────────────────────

Before we move into the framework, I think it's important to say a couple of things about forgiveness.

Where there is opportunity to make amends, the Bible instructs us to do so. There is a story in the Bible in which God tells us to make amends, leave our offering, go make up with our brother, then come back and give our offering (Matthew 5:23-24). But what exactly does making amends look like?

Making amends starts with forgiveness. There are different types of forgiveness. In *Mending the Soul: Understanding and Healing Abuse*, Steven Tracy discusses three types.

The first, judicial forgiveness, involves the cancellation or pardoning of sins by God. It involves confession, the acknowledgment of sin, and repentance. This type of forgiveness can only be requested from, and granted by, God. We seek judicial forgiveness from God in Step 5 through the unbraiding process when we take responsibility for hurts we caused others as a result of our abuse, and ask God to forgive us.

Psychological forgiveness involves letting go of hatred and personal revenge and extending grace to others. We will address this type of forgiveness in Step 6 of the process.

Finally, relational forgiveness involves the restoration of relationships. It is synonymous with reconciliation. This type of forgiveness is always desirable but not always possible. God desires healing and reconciliation both individually—between us and God—and interpersonally—among each other. The goal of a redeemed and harmonious community lies at the heart of God's actions throughout history. We will address restoring relationships in Step 7.

Most of us will never get an apology or know if our abusers have repented in their hearts. Additionally, the people who harmed us may not be accessible to us. In my case, I have no idea the whereabouts of the neighbor or uncle who molested me. It could also be that your abuser is no longer living. Therefore, we will need to lean into God when it comes to forgiving our abusers. We may never know the condition of another's heart, but be encouraged you are only responsible for your own.

As you go through the framework, remember that what happened to you was evil. Recall the Bible tells us we do not fight against flesh and blood but against the evil forces of the unseen, spiritual realm (Ephesians 6:12). People who abuse children are profoundly afflicted spiritually. They are in deep, dark bondage. That's why they did what they did to you.

Remember also that God loves every one of us and came to die for every one of our sins. His love is so much greater than we can ever understand. He hurts for what happened to you as well as for those in such bondage who caused the pain they inflicted on you. This doesn't mean abusers are justified in their evil actions. They made a choice and harmed you and will have to answer to God for their actions.

Forgiveness involves letting go of hatred and personal revenge and extending grace to others. It means that we willingly choose to let go of our desires for revenge and, in place, extend kindness to our enemies. We decide to extend grace based on the grace we ourselves received from God. This is not easy to do. To be sure, "letting go of resentment toward an unrepentant abuser feels like letting go of justice; it may also feel like letting the abuser win and may appear to justify his or her evil."[12]

The simplest way to extend grace in forgiveness is to understand that they have given in to their evil desires and need God's help to break free from the evil that controls them. What we can do for them is understand this and pray for their healing. We can let go of any desire for vengeance and simply turn them over to God. God's love and mercy is so great that even the worst among us can repent, stop hurting people, and experience the transformative love of God.

Romans 12:19 tells us, "Dear friends, never take revenge. Leave that to the righteous anger of God."

"I will take revenge; I will pay them back," says the Lord.
— Romans 12:19

---

[12] Tracey, Steven R. *Mending the Soul: Understanding and Healing All Types of Abuse.* Zondervan, 2008.

Healing is a process, and it can come in surprising ways. Looking back at my past with spiritual eyes helped me to process and release the shame, anger, and guilt I felt. It wasn't easy. There were moments of complete overwhelm. I was triggered and experienced moments of anxiety and dreams. The dreams were unexpected. You may recall that dreams have always been a reflection of my state of mind and the state of my soul. Once I accepted God into my spirit, my dreams changed. That was my season of soaring through the skies. In my time of healing, my dreams were a place where God worked out in me things I didn't dare to confront in my waking hours. God guided me through a process of forgiveness in my dreams. I had three dreams the summer I wrote this book.

I know I'm making progress in this area because I used to fantasize about physically hurting my uncle if I was to run into him, and yet in my dreams, I responded completely opposite from what I thought would happen if I were faced with him suddenly.

THE FIRST DREAM: I LOVE YOU ─────────────

In the first dream, I ran into my uncle at a bar. Why a bar, I have no idea; I have not been to a bar in years. When I saw him, I felt *LOVE.* Yes, love, and disappointment, and I told him so. I said to him, "I loved you. How could you have done that to me?" And then, "I love you." I said it more than once. I don't remember much else from the dream except the love I acknowledged and the love I felt, and that I still feel now. I woke up with the clear realization that I loved him then, and that I love him still. I think I knew that all along, but I couldn't put the words to it because I hated that I felt that way. I thought I needed to hate him. After all, he destroyed so many good things in my life and sent me down a path of darkness. But it's true: He was my favorite uncle. He was kind, generous, affectionate, and fun, so yes, I love him. I believe the ambiguousness we feel about our abusers is one of the most damaging consequences of the experience that further buries us in shame. How could I possibly feel love for him? He's a monster . . . he doesn't deserve it . . . all he gave me was part of a careful plan of manipulation and grooming. It was all very confusing for a time. While what my uncle did to me is not okay, I chose to let go of the pain, to recognize that my uncle was in the grips of darkness when he did those things to me, and to feel love for him. And this all got worked out in my dreams. Forgiveness is a choice we make for ourselves out of gratitude for the forgiveness we received from God.

THE SECOND DREAM: I FORGIVE YOU ——————

In the second dream, my mother had invited us to a baby shower for a child my uncle and his wife were expecting. I decided to go and give him a letter. I wrote out a card intended for the baby shower and inserted the following letter:

> *Uncle,*
>
> *I remember everything you did to me. You sexually abused me and others in our family. There are five children in my family, including me, who I know you abused. Only you and God know if there were even more victims. You left a trail of pain in your path throughout the years. What you did caused me so much pain, anger, fear, and shame. It took many years for me to reach a point when I could even recognize the depth of the pain and its influences in my life.*
>
> ***I forgive you.***
>
> *I no longer desire to hurt you. Vengeance is not for me to complete. I will leave vengeance to the righteous law of God. He is the one who will pay you back for all the evil you have done (Romans 12:19).*

I woke up knowing I needed to write down the dream and prayed the following prayer, wide awake, of my own free will:

> *Father,*

Thank you for a new day. I knew I needed to write this letter. It has been on my mind for weeks. I never expected it to happen in a dream. However, you have been dealing with me in my dreams when it comes to my uncle. Thank You.

My first dream was about love. The second dream was about forgiveness. Forgiveness is an area I have been wrestling with. Even when I started writing my book, I wasn't sure I had forgiven him.

Thank you for the dream. Dreams have always been a language between us, since I was a little girl. Nightmares, flying, and now this.

Thank you for loving me so much that you would accomplish things with me in my dreams that I don't dare confront when I'm awake.

I forgive him.

Lord, wherever he is, whatever his life looks like, and for all that he has done I pray: Open his eyes. Reveal to him what he has done to all the people he hurt throughout the years. Show him the depths of the pain he caused.

Deal with him, Lord, in your Divine and perfect justice. I know that evil does not go unpunished. Encounter him and deal with him, oh perfect Judge of all.

Give him an opportunity to repent. I know that you love him just as much as you love all of us, Father. You sent your Son Jesus as the perfect sacrifice in exchange for all of our sins.

Cleansing and healing are available for him too. I cannot pray for You to forgive him because judicial forgiveness can only be requested directly.

Forgive me for all of my sins, Lord, and help me to be different going forward. Continue to work out my healing and help me to boldly speak of your goodness and power to Your children. In the name of your beautiful Son Jesus,

Amen.

I want you to know that God sees you through and through. He knows exactly what you need and will give it to you when you are ready. Your healing may look different from mine—He has a unique path mapped out for you, but both of our paths lead to the same outcome: love, forgiveness, and freedom.

THE THIRD DREAM: RECONCILIATION AND CAUTION

In the third dream I had about my uncle, there was a devastating earthquake. It felt as though the entire earth shifted in that moment. People took to the streets completely disoriented. I thought of my husband and my kids instantly. I knew I needed to get home to them right away. I sensed it could be weeks before we could leave our home to buy food. I thought, *I'd better pick up some food on my way home.*

I stopped at a small restaurant. As I was getting ready to pay, I turned to my right, and there were my uncle and my stepfather. They offered to help me pay for the food and, after a brief hesitation, I accepted. Surprisingly, I invited them to come back to my home. We bought enough food to feed the family for several days and headed home. As we were headed to my house, I realized I had not let my husband know that I was on my way—with him.

When I woke up, my first thought was: *Seriously? To my house? With him? My children and other children would be there. Why would I dream that? What is God telling me now?*

What I took away from this dream were questions about how and when do we allow people who have hurt us back into our lives, if ever. I know God desires forgiveness and reconciliation, but, unfortunately, reconciliation isn't always possible.

Forgiveness is something that we do for ourselves, internally, for our healing. Forgiveness isn't something we give to others in response to their apologies. The truth is, we will never know the condition of another's heart. Even apologies can be empty and another attempt at manipulation. Reconciliation can only happen when we can see on the outside through their lives that they have been transformed.

I urge you to be cautious about remaining in relationship with abusers. It may not be safe; you can forgive without feeling you have to be in their space. Boundaries are appropriate. We live in a world where, sadly, there is darkness everywhere and it is in many cases disguised and invisible to us. So forgive with a degree of caution. Set appropriate boundaries and be aware that there will always be potential for people to harm one another.

CONVERSATIONS WITH MY PARENTS

Throughout this process, I believe God will provide healing and use the people around you to deliver you from resentment.

My relationship with my mother is a good example of how God is healing my relationship through forgiveness. Before my healing began, I didn't realize that the physical abuse I suffered at the hands of my mother had been equally devastating to me. Once I recognized, acknowledged, and discussed it with her, God began restoring our relationship with one another. When I realized that so many adults had failed to protect me, I was initially angry, but having conversations with my mom about her life and her childhood helped me to forgive her. When I was going through these steps, I had several conversations with my mother about what happened, how she hurt and was unable to protect me. She also told me some of the things that happened in her life. Learning about her experiences helped me to understand that she was also behaving out of her trauma and an unhealed heart. While painful, those conversations brought us closer together and have helped me to forgive her.

We all do the best we can, given our circumstances. Our childhood shapes us in profound ways. Much of what we do is simply based on our "fight-or-flight" instincts. My mother is not perfect. She has made many mistakes, like we all do. My mother was so immature and distracted when I was young that she didn't see the environment she was creating left me vulnerable. She was living out of a sense of survival. The extreme poverty and desperation she lived in as a child shaped her, and survival became her priority. She also gave me life, endured years of abuse, and brought me to this beautiful country with the *hope* of a better life for me. I want to acknowledge that our relationship is not perfect. I choose to give her grace and forgiveness, just as God has forgiven me.

I have not done this yet, but I also plan to have a conversation with my father about all of this. I want to learn about his childhood and what caused him to be abusive toward my mother. He has no idea the pain he caused and the far-reaching effects. We need to have these difficult conversations, in *love*, not in anger and condemnation, but in love and compassion. Perhaps I will get some clarity, closure, or even an apology. I have already forgiven my father. God is so loving and merciful that He provided a way for us to be in relationship even though he was not in my life when I was growing up. I only saw him two or maybe three times between the age of eight and nineteen. His wife was heaven sent. It is because of her and my siblings that I decided I would begin a relationship with him in my adult life. I could not live my life ignoring and avoiding their existence. I am thankful to God for them. None of this could have happened without God's grace and forgiveness. I choose to forgive.

SHOULD YOU ALWAYS CONFRONT YOUR ABUSERS?

What do you do when the abuser is still in the family? Should you always confront them? God will give you the answer to this. You're going to have to really pray about it.

While we don't want to disrupt families and create division, the Bible does call us to confront sin. I personally believe silence protects abusers while leaving children vulnerable. The Bible outlines a process to confront people who hurt us in Matthew 18:15-18:

"If your brother or sister sins, go and point out their fault, just between the two of you. If they listen to you, you have won them over. But if they will not listen, take one or two others along, so that 'every matter may be established by the testimony of two or three witnesses.' If they still refuse to listen, tell it to the Church; and if they refuse to listen even to the Church, treat them as you would a pagan or a tax collector. Truly I tell you, whatever you bind on earth will be bound in heaven, and whatever you loose on earth will be loosed in heaven."
– Matthew 18:15-18 (NIV)

We need to bring light into the dark areas of our lives and expose them for the sake of protecting ourselves and others.

This process also gives them the opportunity to apologize and change. People get really numb to the hurtful things they do, and perhaps they have rationalized their behaviors to the point where they are completely blind to it; we can help to bring them out of that confusion by calling them into reality.

Souls can be restored, relationships can be repaired, safety and purity can be re-established—but it takes faith, courage, and bold action to turn the tide in that direction.

This is, however, not always possible. In my case, for example, I do not know the whereabouts of my uncle and have no way of reaching him. I also would not expose my children to the dangers of a known pedophile. When it comes to confronting and reconciling with people who have abused us, safety must be a priority, ours and that of others. I urge you to be cautious about remaining in relationship with abusers. It may not be safe; you can forgive without feeling you have to be in their space.

Boundaries are appropriate. We live in a world where, sadly, there is darkness everywhere, and it is in many cases, disguised and invisible to us. So forgive with a degree of caution. Set appropriate boundaries and be aware that there will always be potential for people to harm one another. God does not want you to be in an abusive situation. He loves you too much. If you're in a situation like this, I would recommend praying to God for guidance on how to move forward. Trust His leading and don't feel bad about the boundaries you choose to set.

How did I know I had forgiven? There was a moment in which I felt sadness in my heart for the abusers. I felt someone should be reaching out to them and ministering to them, too. I knew I had forgiven when my heart yearned to help in their healing too.

GRACE

Finally, before we begin, I want to mention that God's grace is a gift—we can never earn it; we simply need to choose to accept the gift and walk in it.

God saved you by His grace when you believed.
And you can't take credit for this;
it is a gift from God.
— Ephesians 2:8

Please remember to rest. If at any point, you feel tired, overwhelmed, or anxious, put the book down, take a break, and rest. God may be directing you to sit with certain aspects of your own journey. Deep healing work can be challenging, exhausting, and hard to move through. Don't be discouraged; you probably just need to stop, breathe, and rest for a moment. God works in us even while we sleep.

Now let's walk through the 7 Steps Toward Healing together.

—————————— Contemplation ——————————

In your journal, write the answers to the following questions underneath the words *Desire, Depend,* and *Decide.*

Desire – What do you want to know, heal, or change?
Depend – Is there something you read in this section about relying on God that you would like to bring forward with you?
Decide – What are you going to *do* differently in this area going forward?

Journal your thoughts.

What questions are coming up for you as you read?

Is there anything you are wrestling with God about?

CHAPTER 17

7 Steps Toward Healing

Here are the 7 Steps:

1. Tell someone you trust.
2. Grieve what you lost.
3. Unbraid it.
4. Ask for forgiveness.
5. Accept forgiveness.
6. Abide in forgiveness.
7. Trust again.

DESIRE, DEPEND, DECIDE

*T*hroughout this framework and within each step, the three Ds propel you forward in your healing. The three Ds will pull you to the framework and will get you through each step. If you desire to be healed, depend on Him, and decide to reach for Him, your life will never be the same again.

Step 1 | Tell someone you trust.

What would it look like if we could bare our authentic selves to those around us?
Would they embrace us?
Would they continue to be our friends?

Would they encourage us?
Would they love us still?

Fear keeps us from being honest and vulnerable with one another. It keeps us in a state of hiding our true selves.

When I dove into the process of writing my book, I reached out to a few close girlfriends and asked them if I could talk to them about the work I was launching into. As these conversations evolved, I learned that they, too, had been abused. Within the intimate conversations I had with each of those women whom I had known for years, they found the courage to say, "That happened to me too." Something miraculous happened within those moments that was deeply bonding and revealing. We cried together, prayed together, and comforted each other. Today, those friends and I are closer than ever.

I realized that while we each lived very unique lives, our experiences affected us in similar ways. I found that we held some of the same fears around our children's safety. We also had similar challenges in relationships with our parents, spouses, and friendships that stemmed from our abuse.

When I revealed my story, struggles, and true feelings about the abuse I experienced to a handful of trusted friends, God revealed to me so much about what I lost and gained, the feelings I held about the people who abused me. The broken pieces of my heart came into clear focus when I began to expose and bring light into those areas of my heart.

Those conversations led me to express feelings that I had never acknowledged before. In and through those conversations, God began to reveal to me things I was carrying that I had not realized before and were keeping me bound in shame. He also showed me that I had not forgiven. One day, I heard myself say without hesitation about the abusers, "They can go to the deepest, darkest cave in hell, as far as I'm concerned." That statement stopped me in my tracks. "How could I lead anyone to healing when I hadn't yet forgiven?" I knew I had some work to do in that area. "But, Lord, how do I forgive? What would it look and feel like? How will I know that I have forgiven?" Once I had arrived at that awareness and took my questions to God, there was no turning back. The door was opened, and God would soon show me the way through it. As you read, God answered my forgiveness questions through dreams. We'll do more forgiveness work as we go through the steps.

I remained in this step for a while. Initially, I told my story within the safe space of a journal and eventually to people I love and trust. I reflected on what happened to me countless times. Every time I bought a new journal for the sake of recording my thoughts, feelings, and prayers, the first entry was always about the abuse I experienced throughout my life. Each time I did, I was exhausted at the end and never really kept writing in that journal. Instead, I used it to make notes for work and other things. I see now that I was looking for an outlet. I desperately needed to release the pain, but the process of writing it was so painful that I stopped there and couldn't move beyond that point in my writing and healing.

True healing begins with telling our stories. Journaling is a great way to start this process. Within the safety of a journal, you can be sincere. You may be surprised at what comes out onto the pages. That's your starting point. Even more powerful is telling someone you love and trust.

> *You cannot heal alone in secret. As you step out and boldly say, "Me Too," or "Yo Tambien," you will find comfort and support, and gain new insights. It is within the process of revealing our true selves that healing begins to unfold. Tell your story to someone you trust. Journal insights about your conversation: What did you discuss, feel, and learn?*

Step 2 | Grieve what you lost.

We need to acknowledge our hidden pain and allow ourselves to feel it. Once we are honest with ourselves about it, we have a choice to either hold on to it, take revenge for it, or heal it. If you choose to heal it, grieve what you lost, and give it to God to receive His comfort. This release is the beginning of true emotional healing. Feel . . . grieve . . . turn to God every time . . . in *everything*.

I encourage you to feel your feelings, grieve what you lost, and cry it out to God. There was a moment early in my healing when I found myself leaning into the painful memories of my childhood trauma. Instead of redirecting my thoughts and avoiding my feelings as I had done in the past, I allowed them to overwhelm me. I reflected and prayed—I gave voice to my sorrow and the unanswered questions I had never expressed out loud. The clarity and release that resulted was a pivotal moment in my healing. I emptied my heart and body of the pain I had been hiding for decades, and God comforted me and led me to begin the process of forgiveness.

"As a mother comforts her child, so will I comfort you."
— *Isaiah 66:13*

I was driving to a hair styling appointment one day, when I began to reflect on all that had happened to me. I had a good cry about it that day. What emerged was the most honest prayer I had had with God in my life up until that point.

"God, why did they do that to me?"

"Why didn't anyone notice?"

"Where was their attention when they should have been taking care of me?"

At the end of that prayer, I knew something extraordinary had happened when I cried out to God. Doing so began the next step in my healing process.

Recall that I decided to request my educational transcripts from the Los Angeles Unified School District to gain insight into my childhood. The day my transcripts arrived was another pivotal and challenging day in my healing process. What I saw in those transcripts was confirmation of the turbulent life I had had back then.

In those transcripts I found the addresses where we lived throughout my childhood. We went from Echo Park where we lived with my father to a small apartment in McArthur Park. I attended four schools that year as we moved around, hiding from my father. Being a mother, I know the importance of stability. Transition is hard for children. In those transcripts, I also found the addresses where I lived, in Echo Park, McArthur Park, Koreatown, and Sun Valley where we ultimately ended up.

Next, I decided to search for my uncle who had molested me for years. A Google search quickly produced a photo of a man in a sex offender registry. The man's name was the same as my uncle's middle name. "Perhaps he has taken on a false identity," I thought. He looked overweight and much older than I remembered him. His eyes looked empty, as if there was no emotion left in him. Nonetheless, he resembled the man I knew. The sight of his photo sent me into an anxiety attack. My breath quickened, my heart raced, nearly pounding out of my chest, and I began to tremble uncontrollably.

The sight of his photo as I sat at the table with my children focused on their homework triggered my reaction. I began to shake uncontrollably but did my best to not attract the attention of my girls.

I sent the picture to my sister and mother, asking if it was him. They didn't recognize him.

I texted my husband telling him I was having an anxiety attack at the sight of this man who may or may not be the man who molested me and other children in my family.

That night after dinner, while my children were busy playing in their rooms, I showed my husband the transcripts; he couldn't believe how many addresses and schools colored my first grade journey. I began to open up about my pain and disappointment for all the adults that failed or violated me. I told him what I saw on that piece of paper and what was happening in my life during that time. I started sobbing and revealing in detail the depth of the wounds in my heart.

"Why didn't they protect me?"

"Why didn't they see what was happening to me?"

"Why weren't they outraged when I told them?"

I was in his arms with my broken heart wholly exposed, and I desperately needed him to comfort me as I crumbled into a thousand pieces before his eyes. Reflecting on what had happened to me and telling my husband the details was overwhelming and very revealing. I realized that I felt disappointment and resentment, not only toward the adults who had violated me but also for the people who had failed to protect me. I didn't know the extent of who and what needed to be forgiven. I don't think I would have been prepared in my youth to deal with that knowledge. God never gives us more than we can bear. His timing is perfect. I grieved for all the people who failed to protect me, failed to respond when I told them about the abuse. All the ways in which I cried out for help that went unnoticed. I needed to have that moment with God in which I cried out in pain with my heart broken and bare before Him. I needed to feel the weight of that and grieve what I had lost.

Blessed are those who mourn,
for they will be comforted.
– Matthew 5:4 (NIV)

> *Pray an honest prayer. God can handle it, and He won't hold it against you. He sees you through and through. Nothing you can say will surprise Him. Tell Him how you feel about the abuse you experienced. Ask him your "why" questions. Allow yourself to feel the feelings and verbalize them at His feet. If you feel like crying, let your tears flow; swallow them no more. Imagine you are before your Heavenly Father and hold out your hands in front of you. Give him your pain. It is His; release it. Let it go.*

Step 3 | Unbraid it.

Now we are going to do some work around unbraiding ourselves of shame and guilt.

> **To "unbraid" means to release the shame we feel for the sins committed against us by our abusers from the guilt we feel for the choices we made of our own free will as a result.**

How we do this is through confession, prayer and repentance. The Bible instructs us:

Confess your sins to each other and
pray for each other so that
you may be healed.
—John 5:16

Imagine a braid that contains three separate strands of hair. Braided together, they become one composite piece, making it difficult to see what belongs to which strand. We need to go through a process of unbraiding our spirit of the responsibility we wrongfully assumed from that which we truly own; to release the shame of what was done to us from that which we carry for our own choices and actions. Within the braid metaphor, we have three key players: God, you, and others. God is the only one who can release you from the shame, guilt, and resentment left by your experiences, and thus, He is who separates the strands of the braid. We will develop this concept further in Steps 4 through 6.

Release the shame that does not belong to you.

Abusers are under the influence of their evil desires, to the point that they can no longer control their urges. They are driven by their desires and hardened to the harm they are causing.

What happened to you when you were a child was caused by the evil and sinful choices of others. Those experiences scarred you deeply. They introduced you to sexuality at an age when you were developing your view of yourself and the world. Darkness presented itself and distorted the pure exchange of love and trust that is necessary for healthy human relationships. You desired love and affection as a young child. That was good and necessary for your healthy development during those early stages of your life. Someone gave you the love you were created to desire but also manipulated and took advantage of you. You were not to blame for what happened to you during your childhood. As a child, you did not have the knowledge, maturity, or authority to consent to a physical relationship with someone older than you. They took advantage of your innocence, trust, and vulnerability. It was not your fault; you were not responsible for that. Release the shame you feel for the actions of those who abused you. That is the first part of the unbraiding process. You need to understand and accept that what happened to you was *not your fault*. Those sins belong to the person or people who abused you and God will deal with them directly.

Next, you need to take responsibility for choices you made as a result and deal with your guilt. Although they may have been rooted in the pain of our abuse, we made choices going forward. We need to own them and ask God to forgive us. Were there some actions you took later on in life that stemmed from the abuse you experienced? Is there something in your past that you feel guilty about? That guilt is how we know we have done something wrong. Our guilt convicts us. Celestia Tracy describes it like this: Conviction is the state of being convinced that we have made a mistake and feeling compelled to admit the truth.

> *"If you're feeling conviction about past abuse that you've committed against another, allow this feeling to come. Use it to push you towards confession and repentance. This is God's only remedy for a guilty conscience. The feeling of legitimate guilt is His gift to you so that you will take Him up on His offer to cleanse you from all sin and make you righteous (in right standing) in His sight."[3]*

You were powerless as a child, but as an adult, you can take your power back by releasing responsibility for the sins of others, taking responsibility for yours, and asking God for forgiveness. Here are some practical actions you can take to help you.

Unbraid it: *Release the shame you feel for the sins committed against you by abusers from the guilt you feel for the choices you made of your own free will as a result.*

If you are unsure of where you stand on all of this and need additional help to identify and separate shame that does not belong to you from the guilt that is rightfully yours, ask God to reveal to you the areas of your life being affected by your abuse. Write down any behaviors, attitudes, or actions that have been characteristics of your relationships.

Next, take a piece of paper and separate it into two columns. On one side write the words "Shame that does not belong to me." Make a list of the painful things that happened to you or use your journal entry from Step 1.

Now, imagine yourself sitting in front of the person(s) who abused you. You are free to release to your abusers the shame and blame you have been carrying all these years. It does not belong to you. Return it to the hands of its rightful owner. Imagine this shame and blame in a box you have been carrying, visualize your abuser(s), and hand it back to them. Tell them, "Here—this belongs to you. I am done carrying around this heavy burden. I choose to place it where it rightly belongs." Imagine releasing it to them and walking away.

In the other column write down "My Guilt." Make a list of things you have done that you are not proud of. Pray that God will give you eyes to see the truth. It could be things you did or ways in which you treated people in the past. No one else is going to see this except for you. Be honest.

Now you know. Ask God to forgive you for how you acted as a result of your experience and to help you to be different going forward. Journal your thoughts.

Step 4 | Ask for forgiveness.

This step is about healing the hurt we caused as a result of our wounded hearts. Say I'm sorry. It's okay. You're not perfect and you will make mistakes, but the only way to prevent the pile of emotional baggage we tend to carry with us is to ask for forgiveness.

The night I exposed my soul to my husband, I said things out loud that I had never spoken to anyone. The next thing I knew, I began apologizing to my husband for my misplaced anger and aggression.

"Thank you for loving me."

"Thank you for being patient with me all those years I was angry."

"I'm sorry! I didn't know how to love you."

"I needed to learn how to be a good wife."

"This has taken so much from me: my innocence, my trust in people, and now my life with you, and the purity of motherhood are also tainted with memories."

"It's not fair that I feel ashamed and dirty as I bathe my little girls."

"I'm tired of fighting away the thoughts."

"I'm exhausted."

"It's not fair!"

I can only imagine what a man feels when the woman he loves is hurting so deeply. He held me tightly and began to speak gently.

"It was not your fault."

"You were a child."

"There was nothing you could have done differently."

"Of course, I forgive you."

Being vulnerable with my husband that night unlocked something in my heart. Something miraculous happened as he kissed my tears and told me it wasn't my fault. I needed that outside voice to help me believe it. My relationship with my husband has been different since that night. We are closer than before. He knows me better and is more sensitive to my needs.

We all yearn to be known and loved in all of our messy brokenness, truly unconditionally. We cannot experience unconditional love without first revealing who we truly are.

> *Is there someone who has been hurt by YOU as a result of the pain you carry inside? It could be your husband, children, or a parent. If you are able to apologize to someone you harmed directly, I encourage you to do so. There is so much power in taking responsibility for our actions and asking for forgiveness. Amazing things happen when we feel seen and are still loved exactly as we are, in all of our brokenness. If you are unable to or not ready to have the conversation, write them a letter only you will see and ask God to forgive you.*

Step 5 | Accept forgiveness.

The night I opened up to my husband about my pain resulted in my soul crying out to God and proclaiming His promises over my life desperately.

"Will I ever be FREE from this evil?" I continued.

"Maybe I wasn't meant to experience true happiness untainted by sexual abuse."

"I don't want to live with this my whole life."

What happened next surprised me. I began to say:

"The Bible promises God will cleanse us, heal us, and set us free!"
"He promised redemption, and a full life, here on earth."
"That's what I want for my life! That's what I need!"
"God, I can't do this anymore, I'm exhausted."
"I want to be free. I need him to take this from me!"

Crying out to God in pain that night, and proclaiming His promises over my life, opened my heart to receive the blessing I needed.

I needed to see all of that for what it was: I needed to name my pain and feel my feelings instead of stuffing them deep inside, always trying to be strong. That grief and sincerity as I cried out to God in private, and then again before my husband, were what I needed in order to realize He had already cleansed me. It was in that moment of honesty with myself and God that healing took hold. I woke up the next morning achy and utterly exhausted, but I knew that day that I was knocking on the door of *freedom* and that I would soon walk through it. Hebrews 10:10 was the key that unlocked my chains to set me free. I meditated on those words over and over in the days that followed, "Once for all time." God works fast once you are ready, open, and trusting, hoping, and waiting for him to deliver on His Promises.

Study Hebrews Chapter 10, then meditate on verses 10-14. "For God's will was for us to be made holy by the sacrifice of the body of Jesus Christ, once for all time. Under the old covenant, the priest stands and ministers before the altar day after day, offering the same sacrifices again and again, which can never take away sins. But our High Priest offered himself to God as a single sacrifice for sins, good for all time. Then He sat down in the place of honor at God's right hand. There He waits until his enemies are humbled and made a footstool under his feet. For by that one offering he forever made perfect those who are being made holy" (Hebrews 10:10-14).

GOD chose to take human form and walked this earth so that He could relate to us in all of our pain and weakness. He walked among us for the sole purpose of understanding and taking upon Himself all of our pain and shame. Through His sacrifice on the cross, He made a way for us to come to Him in purity. He took on the punishment for our sin so that we wouldn't have to. No matter what happened to you, He cleansed you on the cross. You only have to accept His grace, and He will make you a new creation through Jesus. It is through choosing Him and inviting Him into your heart that you will receive the transformation you desire.

God is real. He sees you, He hears you, and when you speak to Him, He responds. I have witnessed it firsthand but have no way to convince you. You have to experience it for yourself.

If you have an authentic desire to see him working in your life, tell Him, confess the things you have done that cause you shame, and tell Him your true feelings. Ask Him to reveal His power in a clear and obvious way in your life. Tell Him you want to know He is real, that you want Him to take control of your life and to experience His love fully. We all want to be loved, and He wants to love us. He is just waiting for us to accept His love.

Talk to Him and ask Him to reveal Himself to you in specific ways. Tell Him you want to experience Him and know Him for who He truly is. If you pray this with an open heart and genuinely want it, you will receive. If you are ready to invite Him into your heart, you can pray the prayer right now. Invite Him into your heart, ask Him to make you new, and set you FREE.

Journal your thoughts.

Step 6 | Abide in forgiveness.

Live as if you have been forgiven and forgive others just as God forgave you. Now that you have asked for forgiveness from God and others, and accepted God's forgiveness given to you through Jesus' sacrifice on the cross, you can extend grace and forgiveness to others. Forgiveness is a lifestyle that we must adopt because in this life we will get hurt again; choose forgiveness every time.

When I began this journey into my purpose—getting closer to God, seeking his guidance and purpose for my life, and choosing to walk by faith daily—one of my predominant prayers was that God raise up an army of warriors boldly living their faith out loud. What I didn't know was that God would turn *me* into a warrior. God revealed to me that it was time to share my story and my testimony. I have made a conscious decision to move forward and to walk in forgiveness for the sake of my family and my emotional well-being and because I understand the nature of this world and the source of evil. I don't know why forgiveness doesn't come naturally to us; it should, considering all we have been forgiven. Perhaps it's when we embrace the gift of forgiveness for ourselves that we can begin to give it to others. Until then, we walk around carrying the weight of both our sins and of those who have harmed us.

If that's the case, we must choose forgiveness in order to give it. Then, it would make sense that in order to be set free of the prison of anger and resentment, we must first accept and embrace the gift of forgiveness for ourselves. The Bible tells us, "For God so loved the world that he sent his one and only Son so that all who believe in him shall not die but have eternal life (John 3:16).

Forgiveness is a thread that runs throughout almost every step in this framework because it is the key to true healing, but it's complex and challenging. Most of us will never get an apology or know if our abusers have repented in their hearts. The people who harmed us may not be accessible to us. In my case, I have no idea the whereabouts of the neighbor or uncle who molested me. It could also be that your abuser is no longer living. Therefore, you will need to lean into God when it comes to forgiving your abusers. You may never know the condition of another's heart, but be encouraged that you are only responsible for your own.

Remember that what happened to you was evil. People who abuse children are profoundly afflicted spiritually. They are in deep, dark bondage. That's why they did what they did to you.

For our struggle is not against flesh and blood,
but against the rulers, against the authorities,
against the powers of this dark world
and against the spiritual forces of evil in the heavenly realms.
– Ephesians 6:12 (NIV)

Know also that God loves every one of us and came to die for every one of our sins. His love is so much greater than we can ever understand. He hurts for what happened to you, as well as for those in such bondage that they caused the pain they inflicted on you. This doesn't mean your abusers were justified in their evil actions. They made a choice and harmed you and will have to answer to God for their actions.

Forgiveness is something we do for our own individual healing. Forgiveness involves letting go of hatred and personal revenge and extending grace to others. "Letting go of resentment toward an unrepentant abuser feels like letting go of justice; it may also feel like letting the abuser win and may appear to justify his or her evil."[4] Know that to forgive is not to condone. Forgiveness means that we willingly choose to let go of our desires for revenge and, in the place of that, extend kindness to our enemies. We decide to extend grace based on the grace we ourselves received from God. The simplest way to extend grace in forgiveness is to understand that they gave in to their evil desires and need God's help to break free from the evil that controls them so that they can stop harming people and themselves spiritually. What we can do for them and ourselves is understand this and pray for their healing. We can make a conscious decision to let go of any desire for vengeance and choose to turn them over to God. God's love and mercy is so great that even the worst among us can repent, stop hurting people, and experience the transformative love of God. Scripture instructs us to love our enemies and pray for them (Matthew 5:44).

*Do not take revenge, my friends, but leave
room for God's wrath, for it is written:
"It is mine to avenge; I will repay," says the Lord.*
– Romans 12:19 (NIV)

God is just, and He will rightly repay everyone according to their deeds. God does not take what happened to you lightly. He will avenge you.

If anyone causes one of these little ones—
those who believe in me—to stumble,
it would be better for them to have a large
millstone hung around their neck
and to be drowned in the depths of the sea.
Woe to the world because of the things that cause people to stumble!
Such things must come, but
woe to the person through whom they come!
– Matthew 18:6-7 (NIV)

The Bible calls us to make amends wherever possible. If you are harboring resentment toward a parent or other family member you can have a conversation with, the Bible calls you to address them directly. Have those difficult conversations—do it in love and kindness—and be open and honest about your feelings.

As for the abuser(s)—this is the most difficult step—ask God to release them from the evil that led them to hurt others.

Don't be discouraged if you don't feel like doing this, but I'm going to urge you: Do it anyway. Our words can be the bridge we need. What we confess with our words is powerful. Your heart will follow. Forgiveness is necessary for you to heal. Trust God in this—pray for each other so that you may be healed (James 5:16).

Say or write a prayer for your abuser(s) asking God to help them see the pain they have caused and to lead them to repentance. Ask God to release them from the evil that led them to hurt others and to help you experience true forgiveness and healing.

> *Then, choose to abide in forgiveness each and every day. Make it your lifestyle to give grace freely to yourself and others. We all make mistakes, but we don't have to accumulate pain within us by keeping score of wrong-doing and carrying around the burden of resentment. This active step of abiding in forgiveness will help you to stay free. Choose to forgive yourself, and others, every time.*

Step 7 | Trust again.

Trust, or rather—lack of trust—is one of the more devastating scars left by abuse.

Lack of trust becomes a barrier to . . .

- Building strong or long-lasting friendships

- Taking risks in our personal and professional lives

- And can have destructive effects in marriage and even our experience as mothers

It causes us to . . .

- Build fragile, surface-level friendships

- Play it safe when we should be taking healthy risks

- Struggle to communicate with kindness

- Isolate ourselves and families as a means of self-protection

Lack of trust is extremely limiting to our personal and professional growth. That is why I encourage you to trust again.

Trust isn't easy for those of us who have been hurt, but we must try, with caution and appropriate boundaries, to allow people into our lives to demonstrate and earn our trust in time.

It always amazes me how we can each live uniquely different lives, and yet we process and reflect pain in very similar ways. We were all created by the same God, and, therefore, how we absorb and respond to abuse is universal. When the people closest to us give us love but also take advantage of us, manipulate, and hurt us, it becomes difficult to trust anyone, even ourselves. That makes for a hard and lonely life. The success we desire hinges on our ability to trust God and others. It also requires of us courage and action.

As I shared, I accepted Jesus into my heart when I was eight years old. After I experienced abuse and was left in a state of confusion, two things allowed me to navigate life with strength and hope for the future: faith and support from a few good people. Almost immediately, my life began to change. My problems were not solved overnight, but there was a definite shift in my life. I found comfort in knowing that God was with me. He gave me the strength to confront my life and brought the right people around me to guide and support me. I found myself in the care of educators who not only noticed the turmoil my life was in but also took steps to wrap me in support. The support group I joined was a pivotal moment. There I received comfort and had a safe place to express myself, something I wasn't able to do anywhere else up until that point.

In my adult life I have found the same to be true; God and a few good people continue to be my saving grace. Relationships are difficult when you have been hurt by the people closest to you. Trust can be hard; isolation can feel safer and more comfortable to those of us who have been hurt by others. Honestly, trusting people is an ongoing challenge for me. This affected my relationship with God and with the people around me.

After my daughters were born, I knew I wanted to attend a church. It was important to me that my daughters were raised within a community of believers and that they learn faith and trust in God early in their lives. It was a struggle; I visited several churches, but each time I was faced with needing to leave my baby in the care of strangers while I sat in the services. I knew it would be difficult to focus on the teaching and truly connect with God with my child in my arms cooing and reaching for me the entire time, but I couldn't bear letting them out of my sight with people I had never met before. We visited a few churches as a family but went only once or twice and then gave up. That discomfort was rooted in my inability to trust people and God. It was interfering with my desire to be in relationship with Him and to raise my children under His protection.

Listening to church messages over podcast and worship music in my car was safer and easier. Eventually, my husband told me about a new church that was going to be planted in Hollywood by a young and dynamic pastor and his wife. By now, my daughters were walking and speaking, so it seemed safer for me to leave them in the church's childcare. I'm so glad I made that decision, as the worship was powerful, the message was relevant, and the people were warm, welcoming, and young. Finally, I could attend service, leave my children in the care of the ladies who graciously volunteered to watch and teach them, and reconnect with God. I have to emphasize the importance of finding a church where you are comfortable. When you feel God stirring within you and others, you will grow roots in your faith and into that community.

Boundaries are important. I encourage you to trust with a degree of caution and to set appropriate boundaries. We've got to love and extend grace and compassion, but still be aware that we live in a fallen world where the potential for destruction is all around us and great. We do have to remain alert. The Bible tells us to be alert and of sober mind.

Confronting your past and opening up to others will bring people around you into closer and more meaningful relationship with you. Lean on those people; continue to have authentic and deep conversations with them in love and trust.

We are the body of God.
– Ephesians 1:23

I understand what that means now—not in the abstract sense, but in a practical one. We are His body: His mouth, His eyes, His ears, His hands, and His feet. That is why throughout Scripture He calls us to love, serve, and encourage one another. We are God's representatives on earth.

I praise God for bringing my husband and I together because, through our union, He also gave me my in-laws. They spent nearly twenty years loving and serving our family before I could reciprocate trust and love. The year my husband and I moved into our home, my father-in-law built us a patio cover so that we could have a shaded area in our backyard to play with our babies. At the time, I had just given birth to my youngest daughter. I was on maternity leave with a toddler and a baby. Each day when he arrived, I locked every door and closed every curtain. It was a reflection of my fear of men and lack of trust in people and in God.

My in-laws could have easily taken offense to the walls I put between us, literally. They could have said to themselves, "She's so ungrateful," and closed themselves off to me. They could have told the rest of the family how unwelcoming I was, creating further division in the family. Instead, they continued to love and serve us in whatever we needed or allowed. They never stopped. Year after year, they represented God well and showed me the genuine unconditional love of God. Eventually, I began to trust them. From their example, I also learned to give love to others generously and without condition. I love them and have come to rely on them in so many ways. Their prayers and consistency in our lives have been used by God to bring us closer as a family and ultimately closer to God. By their example, they taught me how to walk with God, be generous, patient, kind, humble, and to seek God in everything.

We were created to live in community, and to give love. God placed us in families for that very reason.

The entire law is summed up in a simple command:
"Love your neighbor as yourself."
– Galatians 5:14 (NIV)

True healing requires that we dare to trust again. Trust is difficult, but you can only begin to trust again when you give people the space to earn your trust. Yes, trust is earned. I am not encouraging you to trust everyone; on the contrary, I encourage you to approach relationships with caution—but do approach them. It's okay to have boundaries. We live in a world where abuse is rampant. It is prudent to exercise caution.

I encourage you to seek out friendships in your community with people in a similar stage of life and to invest in those relationships. Seek quality over quantity. Depending on your personality, you may prefer on-on-one conversations or enjoy small group gatherings. That is the case for me; I still get overwhelmed at large gatherings. I find it difficult to relax if I cannot see what my children are doing, so small groups work best for me. I now have a small group of friends I trust and even lean on for help with my girls.

Dare to trust again, one relationship at a time. God will guide you and bring into your life people who represent Him well, who won't attempt to fix you, and who will not judge you but are there for you to walk side-by-side with you and help carry some of your burden.

As you confide in one person, they will feel safe to confide in you, and as you hold each other up, your burdens will become lighter. You don't have to travel this life in isolation. Healing starts with God, but is sustained by being in relationship with Him and with others. He wants to give you His love through His children.

My prayer for you is that God will bring the right people into your life to love and serve you well. If you have those people in your life already, but struggle to embrace their kindness, extend trust slowly. It's okay to be cautious. Ask God to give you wisdom, to bring the right people around you, and when they arrive: lean on them, seek their guidance, and allow them to love you.

> *By their fruits you will know them:*
> *love, joy, peace, patience, kindness, goodness,*
> *faithfulness, gentleness, and self-control.*
> *— Galatians 5:22 (NIV)*

Now that you have invited God and healing into your life, look for a group or church and commit to being in authentic relationship with people who love and encourage you. Through intimate relationships, you can learn to TRUST AGAIN and REPLACE MEMORIES of the hurt you experienced with new and beautiful ones.

CHAPTER 18

Keeping an Open Dialogue

COMMUNICATION WITH YOUR SPOUSE

I believe God wants to heal every broken area of our lives. He wants to heal all of our broken places, even when we don't realize we are broken. As I mature in my healing and my walk with God, I have begun to experience changes even in my sexuality.

I used to be completely angry during sex, the entire time. There was an angry voice in my head constantly running amok. It would get particularly exacerbated when I didn't have things exactly as I wanted them, even though I never told my husband what I wanted. I struggled to feel pleasure.

Memories of my abuse intruded, completely destroying the intimacy. I spent 90 percent of the time fighting off random thoughts from my past, including the abuse, other experiences I'd had before marriage, and the angry talk.

Things are changing since my healing. The angry talk has been silent for some time, and I don't have to constantly fight off intrusive memories anymore.

In fact, I am beginning to understand sex as the act of worship unto God within the sanctity of marriage that it was designed to be. I know it may sound misplaced to say the words worship, God, and sex all in the same sentence, but consider this: Sex was invented by God. He designed us so that we fit precisely the way we do with our husbands. He put the organs where they are, and He even made it so that we experience pleasure, intimacy, and the release of a hormone that actually bonds us to our partner. God designed sex as protection in marriage, to keep us close and pure (1 Corinthians 7:1-6).

There was a moment when I made love to my husband in complete freedom, for the first time. Not a single thought raised itself up between us. The dialogue in my mind was this, "We are ONE flesh, and as such we have the privilege to enjoy each other without shame or guilt." This pleases God. We are instructed to protect each other by coming together, fulfilling each other's needs.

> *The husband should fulfill his wife's sexual needs, and the wife should fulfill her husband's needs. The wife gives authority over her body to her husband, and the husband gives authority over his body to his wife. Do not deprive each other of sexual relations, unless you both agree to refrain from sexual intimacy for a limited time so you can give yourselves more completely to prayer. Afterward, you should come together again so that Satan won't be able to tempt you because of your lack of self-control.*
> —*1 Corinthians 7:3-5 (NLT)*

I know that God is pleased when I make love to my husband; I am protecting myself and him from outside temptations and getting closer to him through it. It was all designed this way on purpose by God.

This is something that is new to me, and we still have a lot to heal as a couple in this area, but we've come a long way.

The more honest I am with my husband about the abuse, and the more transparent I am with him about the things that remind me of the abuse or that I simply don't like, the more he understands me and protects me.

Ladies, I know it's hard to break out of negative cycles with our husbands, but talking honestly with them is the first step. If you have a loving man who you know would do anything for you, it's time you let him in on these struggles. Most men want to make their wives happy;

they just don't know how and cannot read our minds, so it's going to take some dialogue and education.

I am not encouraging you to share more than you are comfortable with, especially if you are not in a relationship in which you feel completely safe. I cannot overemphasize the importance of this matter: Take baby steps in communication and build up to that deep, open, and honest relationship you desire.

If you do not have a safe and loving partner you can trust, know that God does not want you to be in an abusive relationship. He loves you so dearly and did not create you to be abused by anyone in childhood or in your adult life.

If you are not yet married, know that who you choose to marry is one of THE most important decisions you will EVER make in your life. "It is his primary responsibility as the head of his household to pray for a covering over his wife, his children, and his children's children—down to the fourth generation."[13]

The Lord is longsuffering and abundant in mercy,
forgiving iniquity and transgression; but He by no means
clears the guilty, visiting the iniquity of the fathers on
the children to the third and fourth generation.'
—Numbers 4:18 (NKJV)

Because you have done well in doing what is right in My sight,
your sons shall sit on the throne of Israel to the fourth generation.
—2 Kings 10:30 (NKJV)

Choose wisely, look at his interior, not just his good looks, those will fade; and look not only at his charm, as that will also fade through the stresses and pressures of life (although you can work to keep it alive through mutual effort). Take a good look at his values: What is his

---

[13] Trimm, Dr. Cindy N. *Push: Persevere Until Success Happens Through Prayer*. United States of America: Destiny Image Publishers, Inc., 2014.

relationship with his parents like? How does he treat you when he is stressed or under pressure? How does he treat others? Does he place you and others before himself? Pay close attention and give yourself time to get to know him beyond that early blissful season when a relationship is brand new and has yet to be tested by life. Above all, did he have an early foundation in God? You may need to look at his parents for this one. Do they believe in God? If so, they will have taught your potential spouse Christian values. This matters greatly because those values are needed to form a marriage that will last beyond those early blissful years. The answer to these questions is a glimpse into how he will treat you and your children in the future. If you are in an abusive relationship now, and you know you should end it, do it. God has so much more planned for you, but you need to be in the right spiritual, emotional, and available state for Him to lead you to the place He wants for you.

I am in a very safe marriage. Neither of us was walking by faith when we met. We were focused on anything but God. But early in life, as children, we had that foundation and we would later return to it. Provers 22:6 tells us, "Direct your children onto the right path, and when they are older, they will not leave it." Early in our marriage when we were both drinking heavily, we did have explosive fights, and for that reason our relationship was on-and-off in nature. I knew God didn't want that for me, and I didn't either. Things are very different between us today because we both have God firmly at the center of our lives; we returned to the foundation we learned early on. He is a priority to both of us. We know that a beautiful life can be lived only when we walk in obedience. That is why I can speak so vulnerably to him. I feel secure that he won't exploit it or use it against me.

Do you remember that moment when I talked with my husband and I fell apart, bared myself, and told him all the messy, shameful feelings I was carrying? I got closer to him that day. It's in those intimate moments when we allow ourselves to share with one another that we experience full intimacy. We cannot experience full intimacy and unconditional love unless we let our spouse into those secret places.

My husband and I recently celebrated eighteen years of being together. As a result of my openness with my husband, he has also become more open with me. We had a conversation not long ago in which he also opened up to me more about his life. He was initially afraid to let me into certain places, but he pushed past the fear and vulnerably talked to me about things he had never said out loud. And you know what? I felt nothing but compassion and love for him. We are closer as a result.

Talk to your man. It is only going to make you stronger as a couple.

God placed us in our marriage to love one another unconditionally. You have an opportunity to receive and give, and to grow in your emotional and spiritual strength and capacity.

BUILDING AUTHENTIC RELATIONSHIPS ——————————

When I met one of my closest friends, I wasn't sure we were going to connect. She is a bit younger than me, and I wasn't sure how much we had in common. Early in our relationship, I decided I was going to get to know her and let her get to know me. We quickly began having deep and intimate conversations about our marriages, our struggles in motherhood, and our childhood wounds.

I would never have known how much we have in common had I not made the choice to be honest and to make an effort to nurture this friendship.

We often joke that now that all of our junk is on the table, we really have no choice but to be honest. It sounds silly, but it's true. We made a choice to be honest, and to invest in each other, and as a result, we have become great friends. I still have only a handful of authentically close friends who know exactly who I am, but it started with just letting one person in at a time.

Once I opened up to them and offered my support as they opened up to me, I realized that this is what we need: a safe space to be who we are—the good, the bad, and the ugly. Let's talk about it—*all of it.*

Choose one friend who you feel drawn to and who you know won't judge you, and let them in on your life. Become a safe space for her by first opening up about you, and trust will grow.

Start with one person and watch your friendships transform all around you. Once you experience the freedom and safety of authentic relationships, you're not going to settle for superficial, ingénue conversations and people.

Not everyone will be a safe space—ask God for wisdom and ask Him to bring authentic and loving people around you. He created you to be in safe relationships. When we pray after God's heart, He doesn't take long to respond.

And it could be that you already have people around you who love you and want to support you, but you just couldn't see it before. I cannot stress enough, the importance of appropriate boundaries that protect our children.

PROTECTING OUR CHILDREN

According to research published by Darkness to Light, one out of every ten children will be sexually abused by the age of eighteen. Over 90 percent of sexually abused children are abused by someone known by the child or family. More than 80 percent of childhood sexual abuse incidents occur when children are in isolated, one-on-one situations with adults or other youth. The Crimes Against Children Research Center reports that children are most vulnerable to sexual abuse between the ages of seven and thirteen.

You and I know from personal experience, most cases of childhood sexual abuse do not get reported. I didn't tell anyone what happened to me for years. I thought it was my fault. I had been groomed, manipulated, and kept silent. I was ashamed, confused, and didn't have the words to express or understand it when it was happening. I want to take a moment to give you some encouragement in terms of communicating with your children. I know that you know there is a very real danger that preys on innocent children, and I want to arm you with the confidence to speak to your children openly in an age-appropriate way and to recognize some red flags when you see them.

GROOMING

When I was in kindergarten, my mother sent me to a neighbor's house for help with homework. That neighbor was the teenaged boy who later molested me. He "groomed" me. Grooming consists of gaining the trust of a child and their parents to get access to and exploit a child. I didn't know what he was doing, or why, or that it was wrong. It just made me feel anxious and strange. I didn't have the words or knowledge for any of it then.

If you notice an adult takes great interest in playing with your child, that's a red flag. Keep a watchful eye and trust your instincts. If you are uncomfortable with their interactions with your child, address it immediately. There is no reason for any adult to be overly touchy with your children. For example, if you don't like someone tickling, hugging, or picking them up, tell them it makes you uncomfortable. Take charge and set those boundaries. The worst thing that could happen if you are wrong is that you will have offended a well-meaning adult. They'll get over it. The best thing that could happen is that you will have alerted a predator that you are watching them. Predators usually target children in isolated situations and when they are not being watched closely.

RED FLAGS INDICATING A CHILD COULD BE IN TROUBLE

When I was experiencing abuse as a child, there were many red flags that went unnoticed or unaddressed. I was saying things that didn't make sense to other children. I said I had a boyfriend, I told them I had had sex. I was having violent fights with my brother. I had trouble sleeping and was constantly tattling and lying. These are all red flags. They are an indication that something is wrong. I am not saying that every time a child misbehaves or struggles they are being abused sexually, but something is wrong. It could be other family circumstances causing the behavior. I had witnessed domestic violence in our home, and my parents were going through a very scary divorce. An estimated 3.3 million children witness domestic violence in their homes in the

United States every year. Further, "Children exposed to violence are more likely to abuse drugs and alcohol; suffer from depression, anxiety and post-traumatic disorders; fail or have difficulty in school; and become delinquent and engage in criminal behavior."[14] We cannot assume with certainty the causes for children's troubling behavior, but these should not be ignored either. These should be indictors for us to slow down and pay closer attention. We should nurture an open dialogue with children and provide safe space for them to share their thoughts and experiences, whatever they may be. I want to highlight some of the things that happened in my life that went unnoticed or unaddressed so that you are equipped to respond to the signs of distress exhibited by children experiencing abuse.

There were many cries for help that went unnoticed when I was experiencing abuse that I wish would have been questioned a little more by the adults around me. For example, beginning at the age of about six years old, I began telling children that I had a boyfriend. No one ever questioned it. Had someone asked, "Who?" or "Tell me more about that," perhaps they may have discovered that I had an inappropriate relationship with an older boy—the teenager who molested me when I was five.

Looking back, I recognize that adults had opportunities—and the responsibility—to follow up on comments I made, but didn't.

These are some of the things you can look out for in your children or in other children:

- If the children in your care are saying things that don't make sense, lying, or exhibiting aggressive behavior that cannot be explained, take the time to create a safe environment for them and provide opportunities for them to share in conversation about their lives.
- I know it can be uncomfortable to come into such sensitive information. If you suspect a child is in some kind of distress,

---

[14] "What Are the Statistics of the Abused?" NAASCA, 2011. http://www.naasca.org/2012-Resources/010812-StaisticsOfChildAbuse.htm

it is your responsibility as the adult to ask questions and, if needed, report abuse to people who are required by law to follow up on suspected abuse, such as teachers.

- You may initially want to avoid the whole situation. We have a tendency to want to avoid conflict; we don't want to pry or overstep our boundaries, especially when it comes to someone else's children, but I encourage you to push past that hesitation and discomfort and do it anyway. You could be saving a child from further abuse if something inappropriate is in fact occurring in their lives.

- Don't ever let the fear of having uncomfortable conversations prevent you from asking a question. You could be saving someone's life.

In my life, those moments where I didn't get any validation for what happened, and the lack of response, was really damaging. At that point, I lost trust in the adults around me. It served only to help the abusers because the fact that no one reacted in response to my alarming comments made me think that those things were normal and unimportant. I didn't know it then, but this played a part in my silence going forward.

COMMUNICATION WITH YOUR CHILDREN ─────────

My daughters and I have had an ongoing dialogue since they were toddlers. We talk about small and big things. I look for opportunities to talk and teach them. We have been discussing our bodies since they were toddlers. I talk to them about what's appropriate and inappropriate behavior in terms of their body and personal boundaries. I recently told my daughters about what happened to me. I told them someone had touched me. I told them it was a neighbor and another time it was an uncle.

I told my oldest first. Her eyes got so big and so sad. She put her hands on each of my cheeks, looked into my eyes and said, "I'm sorry, Mami." Then, she hugged me for a long time. I never expected that level of empathy and comfort! My youngest walked over to us, and my daughter looked at me and whispered, "Tell her Mami." Until that moment, I wasn't sure if I wanted to tell her. I didn't want to scare her. But I knew at that point, it was either going to be me or her sister. She was scared when I told her it had been an uncle and a neighbor. Some of their favorite people are their uncle and their neighbor, and I realized that's exactly why it's so important that they know that these things can happen.

While I would love for my children to have remained in a world of princesses and singing animals, I had to confront the truth that they are going to hear things, see things, and experience life. I wanted my children to learn about the sensitive issues of life from me in a safe space where they could ask questions and get accurate information. It broke my heart every time I had to open my children's eyes to the ugly things that happen in the world. I used to fear that by educating them, I might expose them to things they didn't yet understand. I feared I would say too much too soon. I feared I might take their innocence, the very thing I desperately want to protect.

That fear was precisely how I knew I had to take action. In the season of my healing, my children were the exact age I was when it was happening to me. They were at the age in which children are at greatest risk.

I encourage you to create an open line of communication and have an ongoing dialogue with your children about sensitive topics such as this one, so that if or when life unexpectedly happens, they know they can ask or tell you anything and that you will help them through it. As adults, it is our responsibility to protect them.

It's never too early to begin talking to our children about the issue of abuse. Open conversations with children about body safety, sex, and boundaries is one of the best defenses against childhood sexual abuse. I have been talking to my kids about their bodies since they were two years old. Look for teachable moments to introduce the conversation. Don't drop it on them all at once. Just a little at a time as you feel comfortable. Trust your intuition. You will know how much they are prepared to hear and in what manner. They may not understand a lot of what you are saying at first, but the more you contribute to that knowledge, over time the wiser they will become. What's more important, you will set the stage for them to come to you on delicate topics.

EMPOWER THEM AND GIVE THEM THE WORDS ————————

- Talk to them often, even when it's uncomfortable.
- Answer their questions openly and honestly. The only thing they learn when we lie is that their parents lie to them.
- Tell them their bodies belong to God, and that NO ONE, and I mean NO ONE, has the right to touch their private parts, not even their mom or dad (except for sanitary reasons of course).
- Tell them boys have a penis and girls have a vagina. Yes, I know you're cringing! Do it anyway! Normalize the language. Children need the right words to express themselves.
- Talk to them about appropriate and inappropriate touching, playing, and talking.
- Tell them adults are not perfect, and they aren't all good. Give them permission to question and disagree with grownups. I can't stress this enough. Tell them it's okay to tell on grownups. Tell them they will never get in trouble for it and that nothing harmful will happen to them or to the people they love.
- Tell them they are not allowed to play in isolated areas with teenagers. Considering the differences in maturity levels, language, and hormones, there is just no reason for it.
- Walk them through what they should do and say if someone touches them there. Tell them to say, "DON'T TOUCH ME!" Tell them to say it loud and to run and tell a grown up.
- Talk to them about secrets. Tell them it isn't appropriate to keep secrets. Tell them if they have a secret that makes their tummy hurt (children will not recognize this is anxiety), tell them they will feel better by telling you or another adult they trust.
- Finally, if your child says something happened to them, BELIEVE IT AND TAKE ACTION! Children rarely lie about sexual

abuse. Their trust in you, others, and their emotional healing will significantly be impacted by how you handle the situation.

Protect them vigorously at all costs! You will never regret equipping them in this way. You may question how you should say it or if you have said too much. Trust yourself. There are many resources out there to help you protect and educate your children. I will list some resources at the end in an appendix.

─────── Contemplation ───────

In your journal, write the answers to the following questions underneath the words *Desire, Depend,* and *Decide.*

Desire – What do you want to know, heal, or change?
Depend – Is there something you read in this section about relying on God that you would like to bring forward with you?
Decide – What are you going to *do* differently in this area going forward?

Journal your thoughts.

What questions are coming up for you as you read?

Is there anything you are wrestling with God about?

CHAPTER 19

The Path to Purpose

SELF-WORTH

Now that we have walked this journey together up to this point, I'm going to go out on a limb and say: I know you have traveled this life with a void in your heart. You tried to fill it with the things this world says you need. The void you feel is the piece of the beautiful puzzle that is *you*.

God is the glue that bonds all parts of you together, making you strong and secure. You were created to be in relationship with God, and without Him, you're not going to find anything big and pure enough to fill your need. In Him you will find your comfort, your safety, your strength, and your peace.

As you learned, when a little girl receives inappropriate and sexual attention as she is beginning to form concepts of herself, of love, and relationships, she gains a distorted perspective of her self-worth. I learned early on that male attention led to receiving love and affection, in exchange they got access to my body. This was a perversion of God's intention and creation. We were created by God and for God. He cares about our bodies, for they are the temple intended to house His spirit on earth. He created us with love and for love, not for sexual gratification; in fact, sexual immorality, impurity, and greed have no place in the kingdom of God (Ephesians 5:3).

Don't you realize that your bodies are actually parts of Christ?
Should a man take his body, which is part of Christ, and join it
to a prostitute? Never! And don't you realize that if a man joins
himself to a prostitute, he becomes one body with her? For the
Scriptures say, "The two are united into one." But the person who
is joined to the Lord is one spirit with him. Run from sexual sin!
No other sin so clearly affects the body as this one does. For sexual
immorality is a sin against your own body. Don't you realize that
your body is the temple of the Holy Spirit, who lives in you and was
given to you by God? You do not belong to yourself, for God bought
you with a high price. So you must honor God with your body.
1 Corinthians 6:15-20

My childhood experiences left a huge void in my life. I did not receive the support, validation, and unconditional love that children need to become healthy adults. As an adult I sought to fill that void with validation from others, but it never delivered what I truly needed. The compliments and attention I received from men momentarily met my emotional needs. I received a boost from their attentions, and this became a driving force in how I dressed, carried myself, and in many of the choices I made. Seeking attention from men drew to me all the wrong types of men—men who were motivated by their selfish sexual desires. I ended up in some pretty scary situations because of this dynamic.

I once met a man at a nightclub who seemed to be a catch. He was handsome, articulate, and an athlete from a prestigious university. We exchanged numbers that night and, shortly after meeting, he asked me out on a date and took me straight to the beach. Naively I thought, how romantic, he is taking me for a walk by the ocean. He invited me to sit with him on the sand and again, stupidly, I thought, "How sweet." He immediately began to kiss me. I repeatedly asked him to stop as he aggressively kissed me and pulled at my clothing, and he said to me, "What did you think was going to happen here?" He nearly raped me on the beach that night. By the grace of God, he stopped and took me straight back home, which surprised me; I thought he would leave me stranded on the beach. It was one of the most terrifying nights of my adult life. That was not the only time I found myself in that type of a dangerous situation. On another occasion that went almost exactly the same way, I met a man at a club—he was gorgeous—we exchanged numbers, and soon after I received a phone call and an invitation to his apartment. I had another near-rape experience that night.

On other occasions, it was I who flirted and pursued men whom I desired for what they could give me: affection, protection, joy, or pleasure. Each time I gave my body to a man, however, I was only left feeling ashamed, used, and worthless.

I was seeking the approval of men and tying their responses to my self-worth. Each time the results were devastating. You need to know that you are valuable not because of what you have to offer sexually to men but because you were created in the image of GOD, the one and only Creator of the universe (Genesis 1:27). What could be more special than being you? He loves you and made you worthy of selfless love, respect, protection, and affection, and you don't need to give yourself away to receive this.

God is the only One who is going to fill that void for you; the right man, job, house, or car will never come close to filling you up. He is the source of peace and joy that nothing in this world can give you. When you understand and accept that He is your source for all good things, and anything else is an empty replica that will never satisfy you, you will no longer seek validation and worth in others. I love this quote by Brene Brown: "Our worth and our belonging are not negotiated with other people. We carry those inside of our hearts."[15]

Then Christ will make his home in your hearts as you trust in him.
Your roots will grow down into God's love and keep you strong.
Ephesians 3:17 (NLT)

---

[15] Brené Brown Shows You How To "Brave the Wilderness"-https://www.youtube.com/watch?v=A9FopgKyAfI

Honor and majesty surround him; strength and joy fill his dwelling.
1 Chronicles 16:27 (NLT)

You will no longer be blown to and fro in emotional turmoil based on how others perceive or treat you or based on what you have or don't have (Ephesians 4:14). You will be as a house that is planted on a firm foundation.

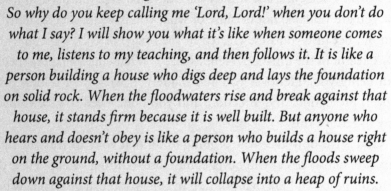

Building on a Solid Foundation
So why do you keep calling me 'Lord, Lord!' when you don't do what I say? I will show you what it's like when someone comes to me, listens to my teaching, and then follows it. It is like a person building a house who digs deep and lays the foundation on solid rock. When the floodwaters rise and break against that house, it stands firm because it is well built. But anyone who hears and doesn't obey is like a person who builds a house right on the ground, without a foundation. When the floods sweep down against that house, it will collapse into a heap of ruins.
Luke 6: 46-49 (NLT)

—————————— Contemplation ——————————

In your journal, write the answers to the following questions underneath the words *Desire, Depend,* and *Decide.*

Desire – What do you want to know, heal, or change?
Depend – Is there something you read in this section about relying on God that you would like to bring forward with you?
Decide – What are you going to *do* differently in this area going forward?

Journal your thoughts.

What questions are coming up for you as you read?

Is there anything you are wrestling with God about?

CHAPTER 20

Walking with God

WHY DO BAD THINGS HAPPEN IN THE PRESENCE OF A GOOD GOD?

I spent years wondering, "Where was God?" I wondered how He could have watched idly as my innocence was stolen, my trust in others killed, and my zeal for life destroyed. I blamed God for failing to protect me. As you read, in my struggle to take control of my life I wound up completely lost and justified my behaviors based on what I had suffered as a child. I reasoned that I simply was who I was because of what had happened to me. I went from experiencing abuse at the hands of others to giving myself away in a desperate pursuit for love and acceptance and making choices that buried me further in shame and anger.

"Bad" things happen, not for lack of love. His love cannot be rightly questioned when we look at the cross. God chose to wrap himself in a human body for the purpose of paying the price for sin that he knew-since the beginning of time-would take hold of us. He created us with free will and knew we would be deceived and broken by the world and someone would have to pay the price. Then He chose to be the one to pay it for us so that we could be joined with Him. He loved us while we were sinners and He makes every attempt to call us back to Him.

GOD'S TIMING

Why did God choose this specific season in my life to bring all of this to fruition?

God's timing is perfect. We don't always understand it, but He has a plan in play even through the hard times.

I believe even the early version of faith I learned served a good purpose. I needed to learn that I was never going to *earn* heaven. Yes, that was a hard, but *good*, lesson to learn. It didn't click for me until recently, but I needed to know that I could rely on Him for everything. I needed to learn that I could not earn salvation. Had I not learned this lesson, I might still be relying on myself to build my life and make it better than the life I was born into. We've seen how I was able to only sort of succeed on the exterior, while inside I was angry, numb, and completely out of control.

God gave me my faith at the precise time when I needed it. He placed me under the instruction of wonderful teachers to come around and support me after the abuse when no one even knew what had happened. He also brought my husband and I together, and through him, placed me in a family that taught me what a healthy marriage looks like. God gave me unconditional love through them. He also gifted me two beautiful children, who ultimately shifted my life by giving me the motivation I needed to truly desire healing. He led me to this time in which I could dive deeply into intimacy with Him. He gave me this dream of becoming an author long ago and brought me into relationship with wonderful friends and mentors whom He used to instruct and care for me in this season of tremendous growth.

He was intent on healing me all along. He gave me everything I needed to heal, and He patiently waited for me to turn toward Him and let Him in, truly, so that He could give me the gift of life He was holding for me all this time. He promised to work all of our experiences for our good, and He always keeps his promises (Romans 8:28).

We all have different ways of getting beaten up, broken, and ultimately enslaved by this world and all the pain it offers. The way out of bondage remains the same. He is the way, the truth and the life, and whoever believes in Him shall be made free (John 14:6).

I wrestled with fear and shame throughout my healing, but I am clear on the fact that it was God who was fighting for me the whole time. The more I addressed, the more I realized I still needed to address. His healing is deep, all-encompassing, and everlasting.

God is good. I see now that He showed up for me time and time again-when I was a child in the form of my mother's boss, moving my grandmother to take me to church with her even when no-one else in my household attended, in the form of the teacher who wrapped me in support in fifth grade, as a stranger at CSUN who invited me to a campus ministry service, through my in-laws who loved me in spite of my defenses, my husband who even in his rebellious years spoke of God's love and saving grace. And, He showed up again when I left my career to help me pick up the pieces of my shattered ego.

How many times has he shown up for you? My guess is that this isn't the first time you heard Him knocking on the door of your heart. Perhaps you were too caught up in your own pain, numb from your lifestyle, or blind from your sin. If you made it all the way to the end of this book pushing through discomfort and heartache I dare to say that He chose this moment to speak to you directly and without distractions.

No matter what has happened to you, He wants to heal you. He is setting you up to *win*—believe it. He loves you like a father loves his little children with tender and compassionate love (Psalms 103:13). He will deliver you from the hurts this life has burdened you with. He wants to take it from you and send it from you as far as the East is from the West (Psalms 103:12), and He will set you free (John 8:36).

ONGOING FAITH ————————————————

Because life is hard and things are going to come at us that we cannot handle on our own, I see the practice of spending time with God like putting on a protective armor for the day. There are seasons in which I get busy and distracted and do not start out my day with God's covering. As a result, I end up getting burdened and depleted.

When we start out our day with God, we tackle the day with Him at the forefront. We are always on His mind, but there is something really powerful when He is also at the forefront in our lives, ongoingly, every day.

Just like in any relationship—within a marriage, for example— there is no one person who can save their marriage all by themselves. It takes both parties doing their part and putting in the work for the relationship to heal and thrive. This is true for our friendships, and it's true for our relationship with God. We are going to need to invest time in each other and communicate often and honestly for the relationship to grow and remain strong.

We are always a work in progress. Self-awareness is the first step to changing. And changing is a process led by God's grace. Healing is a process. Remember that it's less important to know exactly where you are at in the process than it is to know you're heading in the right direction.

There are some effects of my abuse that I'm still working out. Do you remember from my story that anytime there was a lot of stress or discomfort I would intentionally or unintentionally check out? This is called *dissociation*, and it can be one of the long-term impacts of childhood sexual abuse. I could fall back into my mind and look at what was happening from afar without really allowing the conversation or whatever was happening to enter into my mind. There were seasons of my life I couldn't really hear what was going on.

I first realized this in relationships. I would be in conversations and suddenly realize that I had not been paying attention for twenty or thirty minutes, or I would check in and out. Building strong, deep, and long-lasting relationships was impossible as a result.

Even now, there is a lot I don't remember. I didn't know this during those years, but when you shut out the world and close yourself off to the bad stuff, you also shut out the good things. I have entire decades of missed good memories. I remember the awful things because those memories replayed in my mind incessantly, but I missed so much. There were a lot of good things that happened, but I struggle to recall most of my good memories in any detail.

Avoidance is a form of self-reliance. While a protection mechanism, it can be harmful. As you saw for me, avoiding pain and discomfort affected my ability to make lasting friendships, to grow in my career, and even to remember the good things.

Once I became aware of how this coping mechanism was affecting my studies while I was in college, I began to recognize the transition more quickly and could call myself back into the moment so I would stop missing as much at school, in work meetings, and in conversation with others.

Because I knew it was a problem, I became committed to paying attention and worked extra hard on studying on my own, even if I had to read and re-read the material until I felt I had been able to take in the necessary information. It took years of this before I could break the pattern.

I still struggle at times to stay present with my children. There are moments in which I feel overwhelmed and tired and catch myself not paying attention. This is a work in progress for me, but I have come a long way and will continue to fight the urge to disconnect even if it is uncomfortable to stay in the present.

If you resonate with this example from my life, remember that you are more powerful than you think. You can take steps to practice being present. Knowing (awareness) is the first step. Recognizing it is harmful is second, and third is making an effort and choosing to be different.

Allow God to grant you the grace to know that change is a process and He is always working on bringing you to a state of greater alignment with Him.

We will always have work to do in our lives to be better. Life will keep happening, and it won't always be easy. We will experience seasons of pain and disappointment as long as we live on this earth, so we will need to continue to work on ourselves and deepen our faith. Do not be discouraged, because if you accepted Him, invited Him in, and continue to feed the garden of your soul with spiritual vitamins and nutrients, you will be strong enough to withstand whatever storm life brings your way. What's more, you will never be alone in the storm; you will have shelter, and the sun will always rise again.

There will always be more to address as long as you walk this earth. His work won't be completed here, but God has promised to make everything new in due time. That is the promise we should all live for—heaven.

I have set my eyes on heaven. We are promised He will make all things new; He will abolish all evil, sickness, and pain. I'm looking forward to that promise. That is the ultimate goal—salvation.

Once you are "healed," and by that I mean brought into wholeness by God, there will always be a scar where your wounds were. There will be times you will look at those scars and remember. Your memories won't be erased, but they will have lost their grip on your life.

Contemplation

In your journal, write the answers to the following questions underneath the words *Desire, Depend,* and *Decide.*

Desire – What do you want to know, heal, or change?
Depend – Is there something you read in this section about relying on God that you would like to bring forward with you?
Decide – What are you going to *do* differently in this area going forward?

Journal your thoughts.

What questions are coming up for you as you read?

Is there anything you are wrestling with God about?

What happens when we live God's way? He brings gifts into our lives, much the same way that fruit appears in an orchard—things like affection for others, exuberance about life, and serenity. We develop a willingness to stick with things, a sense of compassion in the heart, and a conviction that a basic holiness permeates things and people. We find ourselves involved in loyal commitments, not needing to force our way in life, able to marshal and direct our energies wisely.
– Galatians 5:22-23 (MSG)

Before my healing, I often wondered, "Who would I be if I weren't so angry, if I wasn't carrying around all this pain?" I only recently met that girl. I am completely different today than I was exactly one year ago. I don't get headaches every single day. I am drinking less, praying more, reading my Bible, and choosing and relying on Him daily. I notice people more. I take an interest in their lives and who they are and their needs. I don't snap at my children—as much. I talk to my husband with patience and love, at least most of the time. I don't assume the worst. I am kinder. There is a quiet in my mind and a calm in my body unlike anything I had experienced before. God uprooted my pain, anger, and sin.

The "legacy" of abuse I inherited from past generations is one that I could have easily passed on to my kids but *I will not!* The cycle stops here. I have been set free—I am brand new! I am who *He says I am!* I've had enough of the lies, and I will not go back there again. I have tasted freedom and healing, and I am never going back to the prison He delivered me from.

I hope that after reading my story you recognize that I am not perfect, and I don't have it all figured out. I don't. In fact, this whole season of my life in which healing, passion, and purpose took hold in my life came about when I realized that I didn't have *anything* figured out. My decision to seek God, ask Him for direction, and do things differently going forward changed my life completely.

> *By his divine power, God has given us everything we need for living a godly life. We have received all of this by coming to know him, the one who called us to himself by means of his marvelous glory and excellence. And because of his glory and excellence, he has given us great and precious promises. These are the promises that enable you to share his divine nature and escape the world's corruption caused by human desires.*
> —2 Peter 1:3-4 (NLT)

Remember that if you were abused and you became abusive as a result, Jesus has grace for you! He wants to set you free and make you clean and brand new! That thing you know is wrong; that thing you know you need to change; that thing you wish you could stop doing—He has the power to set you free! Remember as your healing journey continues that it's only in Him and through Him! The choice is yours, you can remain as you are, but know that you will always end up dissatisfied. There is simply nothing else outside of God that can give you the peace, the hope, and the joy you are searching for. There is a cost to following Jesus. You will be challenged to change some things, leave some relationships, and to obey His Word. You will lose some things for sure, but what you will gain will be so much more. Are any of those things worth preserving? If you sat down right now and made a list, no commitment required, of the things you suspect will need to stop or end if you choose to follow Christ and allow Him to take over, is there anything that you wouldn't give to live the life you truly desire?

I've traveled through the dark tunnel where abuse left me. It wasn't easy. I took many detours, but I was never alone. Time and time again, God reached for me. Reaching for Him and holding on was the best decision of my life. He led me through to the other side. The air beyond the tunnel is thinner, and the stresses of life are less overwhelming because I am walking in the goodness and peace of God. Surrendering my life to Him was the best decision I ever made. Addressing my trauma and giving it to God released the built-up tension I was carrying deep inside. As a result, I am more my true self. My husband and children are different, too: They are more relaxed and expressive. The eggshells they were walking on before have been lifted, and they are freer to be themselves. I can embrace them without fear or shame. There is so much more space inside of me now for love, joy, peace, and the memories we are creating in this new season of our lives.

Now don't get me wrong—just because I went through the 7 Steps Toward Healing does not mean that all of my healing is done!

I don't mean to say that I have already achieved these things or that I have already reached perfection. But I press on to possess that perfection for which Christ Jesus first possessed me. No, dear brothers and sisters, I have not achieved it, but I focus on this one thing: Forgetting the past and looking forward to what lies ahead, I press on to reach the end of the race and receive the heavenly prize for which God, through Christ Jesus, is calling us.
—Philippians 3:12-14 (NLT)

There is always more work to do, and more to discover about my relationship with God and His Will for my life. I am learning to trust more and more each day. I have made it a discipline to examine every thought that bubbles up within me and, if it is a toxic thought, I choose daily to bring it into obedience to that which is good instead (2

Corinthians 10:5). It takes effort, but if we want to maintain a peaceful thought-life, and thereby a peaceful home, we need to be intentional and follow the instruction left for us in Scripture.

Fix your thoughts on what is true, and honorable, and right, and pure, and lovely, and admirable. Think about things that are excellent and worthy of praise.
—Philippians 4:8 (NLT)

I am still a work in progress. There are days when the chatter in my mind decides to pick a fight with everyone around me. There are moments when that chatter oozes out and affects the people I love, my husband and children. There are days when I question, "Am I even healed? Why do I still behave this way sometimes?" That's the key word there: sometimes. Sometimes we are going to experience moments of weakness and struggle to be at peace within. That doesn't mean that I am not healed, it doesn't mean that I am not His whom I have chosen to follow, and it doesn't mean that He has forsaken me.

When I arrive at those moments of weakness, it takes extra effort to think good things, say kind words, read my Bible, or say a prayer. Honestly, I just don't feel like doing that in those moments. And that is exactly what I must do. I have to move out of my comfort zone and reach for God—even when I don't feel like it.

Love Is the Greatest
If I could speak all the languages of earth and of angels, but didn't love others, I would only be a noisy gong or a clanging cymbal. If I had the gift of prophecy, and if I understood all of God's secret plans and possessed all knowledge, and if I had such faith that I could move mountains, but didn't love others, I would be nothing. If I gave everything I have to the poor and even sacrificed my body, I could boast about it; but if I didn't love others, I would have gained nothing.

Love is patient and kind. Love is not jealous or boastful or proud or rude. It does not demand its own way. It is not irritable, and it keeps no record of being wronged. It does not rejoice about injustice but rejoices whenever the truth wins out. Love never gives up, never loses faith, is always hopeful, and endures through every circumstance.
—*1 Corinthians 13:1-7 (NLT)*

This scripture challenges me because I don't always behave this way. Then, I remember that it says *love is*, not *Karla is*. I am not perfect, and I will never be perfect. God knows that; He created me.

You will also have moments of weakness, moments when you don't think or speak in a way that honors God. He knew that would happen. Recall Hebrews 10:10; Jesus paid the price for your sin, *once for all time.* There isn't a word, a thought, or a moment that He didn't already know about. He has you covered. You are covered in grace and forgiveness. You will struggle, and sometimes even stumble, but nothing can take away God's love, and nothing can cancel out the price he paid for you. So each time you trip, get up, dust yourself off, and keep moving forward. Read the Bible when you don't feel like it, pray when it doesn't come naturally, be kind when you don't want to be, and trust that God is pleased with you; and if today was a rough day, tomorrow you can start again.

My eyes will watch over them for their good, and I will bring them back to this land. I will build them up and not tear them down; I will plant them and not uproot them. I will give them a heart to know me, that I am the Lord. They will be my people, and I will be their God, for they will return to me with all their heart.
– *Jeremiah 24:6-7 (NIV)*

I have found my purpose in life, and that is to serve Him faithfully, and to lead others to healing. I will continue to tell the story of how God healed me. I will fight to end the cycle of abuse because I know that He is with me. I have seen His transformative power, and I simply cannot keep it to myself because it is available for all of us. *We just need to choose Him.*

I still have a good and loving relationship with my parents, in spite of their decisions and how I was left vulnerable. I realize now that they were distracted by their own struggles, fighting their own battles as best they could, and I got swept up into the darkness that surrounded us in that season of our lives. I'm still processing all of it—we are slowly mending our relationships. The conversations I had with my mom as I wrote this book helped me to reveal things to her that she had no idea I knew as a child—the secrets I kept for her—and how she hurt me unknowingly and unintentionally. That transparency set the tone for her to be more honest and to begin to take responsibility for her own trauma and the choices she made as a result. She is also mending her own heart and her relationship with God. We all do the best we can, given our circumstances. Our childhood shapes us in profound ways. Much of what we do is simply based on our "fight-or-flight" instincts. My mother is not perfect. She has made mistakes, like we all do.

She gave me life, endured years of abuse, and brought me to this beautiful country with the hope of a better life for me. I want to acknowledge that our relationship is not perfect. I choose to give grace and forgiveness, just as God has forgiven me.

My relationship with my father may always be tainted by the past. We have yet to have a heart-to-heart about what I remember, or for him to tell me about his childhood, which probably influenced who he became later. I plan to travel to Texas to visit him and confront those things in love and grace, and I am confident they will repair a lot of what was broken. Perhaps it's never going to be the beautiful father-daughter ideal relationship that I yearned for all these years. That's okay. God's love is among us.

My stepdad was a good man with struggles and demons of his own. He rescued us from my father, provided for us as if we were his own, and never once hit my mother. We only get one mother and father, in my case I have two sets of parents, and thank God. That was for the best. I will always be grateful for that.

What good would it do for my family and I to sit in our pain and anger? Those feelings sit toxically inside and harm only us. I chose to have my own family, as broken, messy, and imperfect as we are, because we live in a broken world and we are all a product of it. I chose forgiveness, vulnerability, honesty, and openness for the sake of peace, purpose, and the life we all have yet to live.

As you continue through your healing, be careful to maintain your garden, making sure you continuously pluck the weeds blown in by the wind. Notice in your garden that even though you plant beautiful plants of all kinds, the wind continues to blow seeds, and those seeds sprout into small weeds. You must maintain that garden, pluck the weeds when you see them, and cast them out. If you do not stay alert in caring and plucking those seeds early, they can grow to the point of killing all the good you worked so hard to plant.

If you were hurt by the Church, I suggest you place that pain where it rightfully belongs: in the hands of the *people* who hurt you.

To you, friend, who were hurt by a parent, I say again, if possible, make amends, and if not, know that the God who led you to this book and gave you the courage to stick with it to the end—He loves your father and your mother so much that He reached for them faithfully and directly. Like a parent, He punishes out of love to give those He loves an opportunity to make things right with Him. For those who have already passed into the next life, I'm certain that God gave them every opportunity possible to give their hearts over to Him. Even up to the last second of his life, Jesus was there, proving that it's never too late to embrace His love. While hanging on the cross, a thief crucified next to Him said, "Jesus, remember me when you come into your Kingdom." Jesus replied, "I assure you, today you will be with me in paradise (Luke 23:42-43, NLT)." God's love for His creation is so great that He is with us even as we take our final breath. I couldn't say with any degree of certainty what transpires in our last moments in our physical body, but

God's love is so immense and surprising that I imagine He shows up one more time to extend his hand to us.

And may you have the power to understand,
as all God's people should, how wide, how long,
how high, and how deep his love is.
– Ephesians 3:18

To the woman who was hurt by someone she trusted, a close friend or relative: I'm sorry that happened to you. You did not deserve it, and it was not your fault!

To the woman whom no one believed. I believe you!

To the girl who no one protected, rescued, comforted, and fought for, the one who didn't get the rightful response the sin offense deserved: I am outraged for you; you deserved to be protected, comforted, and rescued!

God is here with you right now. He loves you. He hurts when you hurt; He cries when you cry. He wants desperately to hold, comfort, and heal you once for all time. Will you let Him?

The Lord appeared to us in the past, saying: "I have loved you with
an everlasting love; I have drawn you with unfailing kindness. I will
build you up again, and you, Virgin Israel, will be rebuilt. Again
you will take up your timbrels and go out to dance with the joyful."
– Jeremiah 31:3-4 (NIV)

And the key to eternal life: Jesus. He will give you the abundant life on earth and guarantee your soul shall never die but instead will live eternally at His side.

"The thief does not come except to steal, and to kill,
and to destroy. I have come that they may have life,
and that they may have it more abundantly."
– John 10:10 (NKJV)

For this is how God loved the world: He gave his
one and only Son, so that everyone who believes in
him will not perish but have eternal life.
– John 3:16

My abuse took so much from me: trust in others, self-confidence, and an appropriate discernment of right and wrong. In their place it left pain, fear, anger, lust, distrust, and self-doubt. These dominated my life for decades; but now, God has mended my heart. Out of the wholeness within me has grown compassion, resilience, trust in God and others, and purpose.

God and the support of a few trustworthy people changed my life for the better when I was a child. As an adult, the love of my family and trusted friends anchored me to the love of God. The support groups I joined during my childhood, and again when I wrote this book, provided a safe space where I could reflect, discuss, process, and ultimately heal from the deep childhood wounds that still haunted me. I knew writing this book would be an emotionally demanding process. I wanted to make sure I had the appropriate spiritual and emotional support I would need when things got hard and I felt triggered or overwhelmed by the process of revisiting my past. I also wanted to be as healthy as possible before I took up the calling of helping others heal. I could not have made it through to the other side without God and the help of a few good people.

THE UNBRAIDED LIFE —————————————————

I created Unbraided Life to support women as they heal the deep wounds left by abuse. You may have been misled by the difficulties life handed you, but you can choose to heal and succeed in life. I want to help you reach for God's healing promises and flourish into the healthy and powerful woman you were created to be. The Unbraided Life is a life in which you have understood your worth, you have released the pain of your past, and embraced the power within you to transform your life, family, and community. The Unbraided Life is available to anyone who desires to be healed, decides to reach for God, and does the necessary work to overcome their trauma. You too can live the Unbraided Life.

Unbraided Life
Live healthy, supported, and free.
Your God-given purpose awaits.

Visit *unbraidedlife.com* to learn more and get connected.

Now all glory to God our Father forever and ever! Amen.
—Philippians 4:8 20 (NLT)

NEXT STEPS

Healing abuse is a process, but you do not have to do it alone. Regardless of where you are in your healing journey, there are a variety of ways in which I would love to support you.

JOIN OUR COMMUNITY!

INDIVIDUAL COACHING: If you would like additional support as you walk through your 7 Steps Toward Healing, I am available to support you one-on-one as you work through this process. Individual coaching offers a safe space to reflect, discuss, and walk through the steps in partnership with me as your safe, committed listener.

GROUP COACHING: You might be interested in joining one of my groups. This is a fantastic way to connect with others on a similar journey, receive guidance for your healing, and give and receive support and encouragement. These groups are also an exercise in building trust and healthy relationships, and are an opportunity to create positive memories.

FOR ORGANIZATIONS: Workshops, individual and group coaching packages are available. To bring 7 Steps Toward Healing to your organization, contact 7steps@unbraidedlife.com or visit UnbraidedLife.com.

Below you will find a list of books, podcasts, and other resources that were instrumental in my healing journey, as well as some knowledge about how they helped me to step boldly into my purpose—the important and much needed work of helping people heal. You can also find links to all of these resources at my website: www.unbraidedlife.com.

Books

Mending the Soul: Understanding and Healing Abuse by Steven R. Tracy provided an in depth biblically and psychologically informed view of the various types of abuse, its effects, and a path to healing within a safe community. As I wrote this book, I participated in a women's support group with Mending the Soul that helped me to process all that I was experiencing and learning.
www.mendingthesoul.org

Playing Big: Finding Your Voice, Your Mission, and Your Message by Tara Mohr helped me to silence the anger-fueled chatter in my mind, push through fear, and step courageously into my purpose.
www.taramohr.com

Sex, Jesus, and the Conversations the Church Forgot by Mo Isom was an important read for me in my season of healing. Writing about my sexual sin was one of the hardest things I have ever done. Isom's transparency and vulnerability helped me to push through the fear of judgment I felt at times and helped me to learn a godly perspective on sexual intimacy in marriage.
www.moisom.com

Gay Girl, Good God by Jackie Hill Perry gave me the courage to vulnerably and honestly discuss my same sex attraction.
www.jackihillperry.com

Healing the Soul of A Woman by Joyce Meyer confronted my bitterness and struggle with anger and challenged me to continue doing the hard work of healing.
www.joycemeyer.org

Rising Strong: How The Ability to Reset Transforms How We Live, Love, Parent, and Lead by Brene Brown, PhD, LMSW confirmed everything I learned from personal experiences about the power of vulnerability to set us free from shame.
www.brenebrown.com

Think, Learn, Succeed: Understanding and Using Your Mind to Thrive at School, the Workplace, and Life and Switch on Your Brain by Dr. Caroline Leaf provided scientific and biblical truth about the formation of memories and the power we have to heal our brain with our minds.
www.drleaf.com

Whisper: How to Hear the Voice of God by Mark Batterson taught me a lot about what God's voice is and isn't.
www.markbatterson.com

Podcasts
Dr. Caroline Leaf's podcast on mental health issues provides tools and tips to equip and empower you to overcome mental health issues.
www.drleaf.com

Misa Leonessa's podcast "Beyond Abuse Radio" shares about finding God in the midst of trauma healing. While this podcast is older and no longer active, I found it tremendously insightful during my season of intense healing.
www.misacoach.com

Support Group
Mending the Soul: Understanding and Healing Abuse Women's Small Group provide a safe space to reflect, learn, and heal within a safe community of like-minded women.
www.mendingthesoul.org

Coaching
Unbraided Life provides individual and group coaching to help women heal from trauma within a safe and supportive community. www.unbraidedlife.com

Noteworthy Lab provided guidance, reassurance, and an environment of discovery that led me to pursue my life-long dream of becoming a published author and coach.
www.noteworthylab.com

Darkness to Light is a nonprofit dedicated to preventing childhood sexual abuse.
www.d2l.org

──────────── Recommended Resources ────────────

Courage and Purpose

Whisper: How to Hear the Voice of God
by Mark Batterson

Playing Big: Finding Your Voice, Your Mission, and Your Message
by Tara Mohr

*Rising Strong: How The Ability to Reset Transforms
How We Live, Love, Parent, and Lead*
by Brene Brown, PhD, LMSW

Healing

Mending the Soul: Understanding and Healing Abuse
by Steven R. Tracy

Healing the Soul of A Woman
by Joyce Meyer

*Think, Learn, Succeed: Understanding and Using Your
Mind to Thrive at School, the Workplace, and Life*
by Dr. Caroline Leaf

*Switch on Your Brain: The Key to Peak Happiness,
Thinking, and Health*
by Dr. Caroline Leaf

Marriage

Love & Respect
by Emerson Eggerichs

Sacred Marriage
by Gary Thomas

Sexuality

*Gay Girl, Good God: The Story of Who I Was
and Who God Has Always Been*
by Jackie Hill Perry

Sex, Jesus, and the Conversations the Church Forgot
by Mo Isom

Spirituality

Imagine Heaven
by John Burke

Podcasts

Dr. Caroline Leaf Podcast

Beyond Abuse Radio

Don't Mom Alone

Thriving Beyond Belief

The Porch

References

Batterson, Mark. *Whisper: How to Hear the Voice of God*. United States of America: Multnomah, 2017.

"Childhood Sexual Abuse Statistics." Darkness to Light. Accessed June 20, 2018. https://www.d2l.org/the-issue/statistics/.

Leaf, Dr. Caroline. *The Perfect You: A Blueprint for Identity*. United States of America: Baker Books, 2017.

Leaf, Dr. Caroline. *Think Learn Succeed: Understanding and Using Your Mind to Thrive at School, the Workplace, and Life*. United States of America: Baker Books, 2018.

Leaf, Dr. Caroline. *Switch on Your Brain: The Key to Peak Happiness, Thinking, and Health*. United States of America: Baker Books, 2013.

Meyer, Joyce. *Healing the Soul of a Woman: How to Overcome Your Emotional Wounds*. United States of America: Faith Words: 2018.

Peterson, Eugene H. *The Message Remix: The Bible in Contemporary Language*. Colorado Springs, Colorado: NavPress Publishing Group, 2003.

Tracy, Celestia G. *Mending the Soul Workbook for Men and Women*. United States of America: Mending the Soul Ministries, 2012.

Tracy, Steven R. *Mending the Soul: Understanding and Healing Abuse*. United States of America: Zondervan, 2005.

Trimm, Cindy N. *Push: Persevere Until Success Happens Through Prayer*. United States of America: Destiny Image Publishers, 2014.

"What Are the Statistics of the Abused?" National Association of Adult Survivors of Child Abuse. Accessed June 20, 2018. http://www.naasca. org/2012-Resources/010812-StaisticsOfChildAbuse.htm.

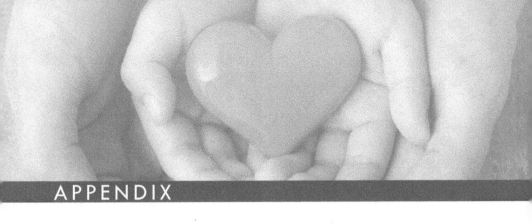

ADDITIONAL SUPPORT

Clickable resources are also available at unbraidedlife.com.

No one deserves to experience abuse of any kind, for any reason.

If you suspect that a child has been, or is in danger of, abuse or neglect, CONTACT YOUR COUNTY'S CHILDREN'S PROTECTIVE SERVICES 24-HOUR EMERGENCY RESPONSE PHONE. You may also contact the police or county sheriff. http://www. cdss.ca.gov/Reporting/Report-Abuse/Child-Protective-Services/ Report-Child-Abuse

Abuse can take many forms.

If you are unsure if you are currently in an abusive relationship, LEARN ABOUT THE VARIOUS TYPES OF DOMESTIC VIOLENCE HERE. https://www.thehotline.org/is-this-abuse/abuse-defined/

If you have concerns about what's happening in your relationship, get help. Contact the National Domestic Violence Hotline by phone at 1-800-799-SAFE (7233), or 1-800-787-3224 (TTY).

The National Sexual Assault Hotline is also free, confidential, and available 24 hours each day. Call (800) 656-HOPE. https://www.rainn. org/safety-prevention.

Karla Monterrosa, M.P.A. is an author, keynote speaker, and women's empowerment coach who has dedicated her life to improving the lives of women and families. She earned a Bachelor of Arts in Urban Studies and Planning and a Master of Public Administration in Public Sector Management and Leadership from California State University, Northridge.

Karla began her career in the City of Los Angeles, where she quickly became aware of the scale of challenges that large, diverse communities face. She learned how to address needs by best utilizing what was already available and, during her tenure, helped to provide women, youth, and families with programming that increased financial literacy, education, and economic opportunities. Karla's ability to pinpoint trauma and develop strategic solutions would serve as the launching pad to her own coaching program, Unbraided Life (www.unbraidedlife.com).

A survivor of abuse herself, Karla is passionate about leveraging her skills to help others overcome their past. She specializes in guiding women to discover their God-given purpose through honest self-reflection, application of biblical principles, and her one-of-a-kind 7 Steps Toward Healing framework.

Karla is a certified Mending the Soul support group facilitator, but it's her almost two decades of experience in community and economic development that make her programming practical, unique, and transformational.

You can find Karla on these platforms:

Web: www.unbraidedlife.com
Instagram: @karlabmonterrosa
Facebook: Karla Monterrosa

To book Karla to speak: speaking@unbraidedlife.com.

A sample of keynote topics she offers:
7 Steps Toward Healing
Marriage, Motherhood, and Memories
Breaking the Cycle of Abuse
The Path to Purpose

CPSIA information can be obtained
at www.ICGtesting.com
Printed in the USA
LVHW021002081019
633522LV00011B/454/P